Sparks Create Change

Based On True Events

Nicole Chanel

Dedication

Dedicated to Glenda

For teaching me what love truly is and for being the reason I learned to hope. Your quiet strength, boundless compassion, and unwavering belief in me have been the light that guided me through the darkest moments. You taught me how to navigate through difficult times, the power of forgiveness, and the courage to continue to fight — continue to live and keep moving forward when the world seems unbearable.

And to all the lives we've lost to violence and trauma— this is for them. For the voices that were silenced too soon, for the hearts that were broken, and for the futures that were stolen. May this book serve as a testament to their memories, a voice for the voiceless, and a spark of hope for survivors who carry the weight of their pain but refuse to let it define them.

This is a love letter to those who have suffered, a reminder that healing is possible, and a promise that their stories will not be forgotten.

Acknowledgment

This book emerged from the depths of my personal journey. It serves as a testament to survival, resilience, and the unwavering hope that guided me through my darkest moments. As I share my story, I acknowledge, first and foremost, the strength within myself that I never knew existed until I was forced to find it.

To every victim of violence who has ever felt silenced, isolated, or afraid, I assure you, your pain is seen, your strength is recognized, and your story matters. This book is my way of reaching out, of creating a bridge between survival and triumph, between trauma and healing.

I acknowledge the power of hope—not just as an emotion but as a lifeline that pulled me through when nothing else could. It was hope that whispered to me about the possibility of turning my pain into purpose, of using my story to ignite change in the lives of others who walk similar paths.

To those who may find these pages in their moments of need, I want you to know that you are not alone. Our stories, though born from darkness, can become beacons of light for others. Every word written here carries the intention of sparking change, of transforming victims into survivors, and survivors into warriors for change.

I acknowledge the collective strength we hold when we stand together. Through sharing our stories, we weave a fabric of resilience that can wrap around and support others who are still finding their way. Together, we are not just stronger, but we are unstoppable.

This book is dedicated to the journey of healing, to the power of transformation, and to every single person who will use their story to create change. Remember: through strength comes healing, and through healing comes the power to change not only our own lives but the lives of those around us.

With hope and determination,

Nicole Chanel

March 2025

CONTENTS

About the Author

Nicole Chanel — A Survivor. Leader. Change Maker.

From the depths of adversity to the heights of executive leadership, Nicole Chanel's journey embodies the transformative power of resilience and unwavering determination. As a survivor of violence who refused to let her story end in darkness, Nicole has channeled her experiences into a mission that transcends traditional business success. She has proven herself to be an individual who people can look up to, providing them with a beacon of hope in their fight against violence and the battles they fight in silence.

With over two decades of executive-level experience in healthcare operations and business development, Nicole has masterfully merged her professional expertise with her personal calling. Her career achievements span state and national healthcare operations, where she has consistently driven excellence through innovative marketing strategies and operational transformations. However, it's her personal journey of survival and triumph that gives these accomplishments their deepest meaning.

Her approach to business strategy is infused with an authentic understanding of human resilience. She possesses a quality that sets her apart in developing programs that truly impact lives.

As the driving force behind Sparks Create Change, Nicole leverages her comprehensive background in digital and social media marketing to amplify voices that need to be heard. Her expertise in navigating complex regulatory landscapes is matched only by her ability to navigate the elaborate paths of healing and empowerment. Every strategic partnership she develops, every operational process she streamlines, serves a greater purpose: creating accessible pathways to freedom and healing for victims of violence.

Nicole's commitment to excellence extends far beyond traditional metrics of success. While her professional achievements include significant cost savings, improved outcomes, and expanded market reach, her true measure of success lies in the lives she touches and the changes she inspires. Her data-driven approach to business is balanced with a deeply personal understanding of what it means to transform pain into power.

Today, Nicole stands as a testament to the possibility of not just surviving but thriving. She represents the convergence of professional excellence and personal purpose, using her platform to ensure that no victim of violence walks alone. Her strategic acumen matches her unrelenting dedication to creating change in making that change sustainable and far-reaching.

Whether she's leading multi-state operations or reaching out to individual survivors, Nicole brings the same passionate intensity and unwavering commitment to excellence. Her story is not just one of personal triumph—it's a powerful reminder that with hope, determination, and the right support, anyone can transform their circumstances and create meaningful change in the world.

Nicole continues to push boundaries and break down barriers, ensuring that every life touched by violence has access to the resources, support, and hope needed for transformation. Her work through Sparks Create Change represents her ultimate vision: a world where survival stories become success stories and where every victim finds their path to becoming a victor.

"Through strength comes healing, and through healing comes the power to change not only our own lives but the lives of those around us." — Nicole Chanel

Chapter 1:
Born into Winter

The February morning was bitter, the air sharp with the cold. Snow dusted the windows of the small Texas hospital where Michele came into the world at 6:47 AM. There she was, making the hospital halls echo with her first cries, halls that smelled of antiseptic and stale coffee. Outside, the winter blizzard that had battered the region for days continued its assault, much like the storm brewing within the hospital room where Glenda cradled her newborn daughter.

Harold stood at the window, his broad shoulders tense beneath his police uniform, still on duty despite his daughter's birth. The fluorescent lights caught his badge, and as they did, they sent sharp reflections across the room. It was a reminder of the authority he carried everywhere — even here, in what should have been a moment of pure joy. His presence felt more like surveillance than celebration.

Glenda, exhausted from twenty hours of labor, held Michele close to her chest. She watched her newborn with love unmatched by any other. It was as if the mother was memorizing every detail of her daughter's face. The baby's skin was still mottled from birth, her tiny fingers curled into fists, dark hair damp against her head. In that moment, Glenda experienced a love so profound it brought tears to her eyes—a fierce, protective love she had never known possible.

"She's perfect," Glenda whispered, more to herself than to Harold.

His response was a grunt, followed by the sharp snap of his leather holster as he adjusted his gun belt. "Another mouth to feed," he muttered, already turning toward the door. "I've got to get back to the station. The chief's short-handed with this weather."

The door clicked shut behind him. and so it was now Glenda and her daughter and the steady beep of hospital monitors. When the mother and the daughter were left alone, they spoke, not in words but in a bond only a mother and a child shared. She then gently pressed her lips to Michele's forehead, making a silent promise: "I'll protect you, little one. No matter what it takes."

The nursing staff noticed Harold's absence during their rounds, their sympathetic glances speaking volumes. They had seen his type before—law enforcement officers whose authority at work bled into their home lives, whose need for control manifested in subtle cruelties. One nurse, older than the rest, lingered longer than necessary, adjusting Glenda's pillows and checking Michele's swaddling.

"You've got a fighter here," the nurse said softly, noting how the newborn gripped her finger. Then, lower still, "The social worker's number is on the back of your discharge papers. Just in case."

The shadows of Harold's past haunted their small house on Cedar Street from the moment they brought Michele home. His service in Vietnam had left more than physical scars, for it had carved darkness into his soul that seeped into every corner of their lives. The police scanner he installed in the nursery filled their nights with a constant stream of violence and crisis, its crackle underlying Michele's infant cries.

"She needs to learn what the real world sounds like," he insisted when Glenda tried to move the scanner. "No daughter of mine is growing up soft."

At night, his screams would wake Michele. Her tiny body would as Glenda would rush to quiet her before the sound could fully rouse him. The baby learned early to cry without noise, a skill that would serve her too well in years to come.

Harold's position in law enforcement created a web of surveillance that trapped them long before Glenda recognized it as such. His fellow officers became unwitting spies. It involved their routine patrols doubling as welfare checks on his family.

"Saw your wife at the grocery store today," they'd mention during shift changes. "Little one was fussy. Everything okay at home?"

Each casual observation became a note in Harold's mental ledger. It served as ammunition for the interrogations that inevitably followed. He tracked their movements exactly how police would — with great precision. He would also cross-reference times and locations like he was working a case.

"Johnson saw you at the park at 2:15," he'd say over dinner, voice casual but eyes sharp. "Didn't get home until 4:30. Where were those other two hours, Glenda?"

The nuclear power plant where Glenda found work as a cleaning contractor seemed like an escape at first. Harold approved because several officers moonlighted there as security, keeping her under what he called "protective surveillance." The late-night shifts gave her precious hours of freedom, but at a cost, she wouldn't understand until years later.

"Just a sore throat," she'd tell Michele when the coughing started, not knowing the exposure was already settling into her bones. "The cleaning chemicals are strong here."

Michele learned to read the atmosphere of their home like a weather report. The way Harold hung his gun belt told her what kind of night it would be. Clean and precise meant danger, casually dropped meant he'd started drinking early. She cataloged these details with a child's desperate need to predict storms.

"Baby, go play in your room," Glenda would whisper, recognizing the signs. "Remember our quiet game? Let's see how long you can stay extra quiet tonight."

Their public image required constant maintenance. Harold insisted on regular family photographs, perfectly staged scenes of domestic bliss. He kept them displayed at the police station as an evidence of his exemplary home life, exhibits in a case he was always preparing against accusations that might come.

"Such a beautiful family," his colleagues' wives would coo during department gatherings. "You're so lucky, Glenda."

Luck had nothing to do with it. Every smile in those photos was choreographed, every pose designed to hide bruises and fear. Michele learned to perform her role flawlessly, which primarily involved being the adoring daughter of a respected officer. She watched her mother do the same, understanding even at four that survival sometimes looked like submission.

The daycare became another checkpoint in Harold's surveillance network. The director, Mrs. Patel, noticed Michele's increasing withdrawal, her startled reactions to loud noises, the way she flinched when adults moved too quickly near her. But Harold had already established their narrative.

"Her mother's family has a history of nervous conditions," he explained during a parent conference, his badge prominently displayed on his belt. "We're working with a specialist. Thank you for your concern, but we have it handled."

It was never brought up by Mrs. Patel. However, that did not mean that she stopped what she was doing. She still kept an eye, observing whatever it was that unfolded before her eyes. She even started keeping a private file of her observations. Years later, that documentation would help build the case that finally freed them.

The catalyst came on Michele's fifth birthday. Harold insisted on hosting a party at their house. He wanted it to be a proper celebration with Michele's kindergarten class and other officers' children, a perfect display of normal family life. Amidst all this, Glenda knew she had eyes on her. She spent days preparing, knowing every detail would be scrutinized by the law enforcement wives who served as Harold's unofficial inspection team.

The party itself was a masterpiece of pretense. Harold played the devoted father, helping Michele open presents, serving cake with steady hands despite starting his drinking at dawn. He wore his uniform, though off-duty—the badge a constant reminder of his authority, even here among children's laughter and birthday songs.

When one of Michele's classmates accidentally spilled juice on the new carpet, the facade cracked. Glenda saw it happen in slow motion: the cup falling, the red punch spreading, Harold's face transforming from a public mask to a monster he had always been in private.

"Everybody out!" His voice carried that familiar edge that made Michele instinctively move closer to her mother. "Party's over. Michele's not feeling well."

Parents gathered their children quickly, for they were trained by small-town politics to ignore the tension. Only Officer Martinez's wife lingered, her eyes meeting Glenda's with uncomfortable recognition.

"Call if you need anything," she whispered, pressing a piece of paper into Glenda's hand as she left. Later, Glenda would find it was a domestic violence advocate's direct number—one that couldn't be traced through police channels.

What followed haunted Michele's nightmares for years. Harold's rage exploded not at her or Glenda but at the pile of birthday presents. He methodically destroyed each one, turning the destruction into a lesson about order and control.

"Watch closely," he instructed Michele, his voice terrifyingly calm as he ripped apart Mr. Hoppy, her beloved stuffed rabbit. "This is what happens when you let people make messes in Daddy's house. This is what happens when you can't maintain proper discipline."

The word "discipline" had a special meaning in their home. It was Harold's favorite justification, the shield he used to transform abuse into authority. He'd learned it in the police academy, refined it in Vietnam, and perfected it at home.

Glenda found Michele hours later, trying to sew Mr. Hoppy back together with her small hands, tears falling silently on the torn fabric. The scene crystallized something Glenda had been slowly realizing. Michele was learning to process pain the way she'd watched her mother do—quietly, carefully, hiding all evidence of weakness.

That night, after Harold left for his shift, Glenda made her first call to the advocate's number. The questions were direct: Do you have somewhere to go? Can you get to money? Does he monitor your car's mileage? Does he have access to license plate readers, traffic cameras, police databases?

"I need time," Glenda whispered into the phone, watching Michele sleep. "I need to do this right. He has too many friends here. We'll only get one chance."

The planning took months. Glenda created a system of dead drops with the advocate, leaving notes in library books, receiving information through grocery store receipts. She memorized patrol schedules, shift changes, the rotation of dispatchers who might or might not report suspicious activity.

The nuclear plant job became crucial to their escape plan. Glenda volunteered for extra shifts, carefully building a reputation for working late. The security guards, all former or moonlighting officers, grew used to her presence. They stopped logging her exact hours, a small oversight that gave her precious windows of unaccounted time.

Michele became her silent partner in escape. At five, she understood instinctively what was at stake. She learned to pack a bag without disturbing the precise order of her closet, to memorize phone numbers through songs, to create diversions when Harold's suspicions rose.

"Such a Daddy's girl," he would praise as Michele asked for extra bedtime stories on nights when Glenda needed to move money or supplies. "Not like your mama, always sneaking around."

The irony was that Harold's own police training had taught them how to evade him. Glenda learned from his casual comments about surveillance techniques, about how domestic violence victims were tracked, about the mistakes that got runners caught. She used his lessons against him, building their escape route around the blind spots in law enforcement protocols.

The final straw came during a routine traffic stop. Officer Rogers, one of Harold's closest friends on the force, pulled Glenda over for a "broken tail light." His real message was clear.

"Harold's concerned about your late hours," Rogers said, hand resting meaningfully on his weapon. "Says you might be thinking of doing something stupid. Remember... this is a small town. People talk."

That night, Glenda made their final preparations. She waited until Harold's breathing indicated deep sleep, then slipped Michele's baby album and their essential documents into her vacuum cleaner's dust compartment—the one place Harold never checked. Each paper represented a piece of their future: birth certificates, immunization records, school documents, all carefully cleaned of any traceable marks or electronic tags.

They left on a Sunday morning during Harold's sleep-off after a night shift. The timing was deliberate—most of his fellow officers would be in church or recovering from their own late shifts. Glenda had prepared Michele for weeks, making it into a game.

"Remember, baby," she whispered as they loaded the car in the pre-dawn darkness. "Just like we practiced. Quiet as mice until we cross the state line."

Michele clutched a new Mr. Hoppy, the one purchased in secret, kept hidden until this moment. The old one, still bearing the scars of Harold's birthday rage, they left behind as a message.

Their departure looked like any other Sunday morning errand. Glenda had carefully maintained this pattern for months: early grocery shopping while Harold slept, Michele dressed in her church clothes as though they'd attend the later service.

But today, they drove past the grocery store, past the church, past the town limits. Glenda watched the rearview mirror, her hands steady on the wheel despite her racing heart. Every patrol car they passed triggered a silent prayer.

They switched cars at a pre-arranged spot—a storage facility where Glenda had parked a used Honda weeks earlier, paid for in cash. The advocate had helped arrange the purchase through a women's shelter network.

"Leave anything he might have touched," Glenda

instructed as they transferred their essential bags. "He knows people who can track us through the smallest things."

Their old car would be picked up and later driven to a different state to create a false trail. The advocate had thought of everything, using experience bought with other women's failed attempts at freedom.

It was a three-day drive to Montana, but it felt like an eternity. They stayed off main highways, used cash only, slept in small motels under false names. Glenda knew she had to chang their appearance, which she did — subtly, of course at each stop that they found on their way. The change involved cutting Michele's hair shorter, dying her own darker, switching clothes bought from roadside thrift stores.

Michele watched her mother transform them mile by mile. It was a desperate attempt to erase traces of their old life. "Are we playing pretend?" she asked at one stop, trying on her new persona like a game.

"We're being butterflies," Glenda explained, helping her practice their new names. "Sometimes you have to change completely to be free."

They arrived in Whitefish, Montana, as the sun set behind the snow-capped mountains. The landscape was alien to their Texan eyes, though harsh but beautiful. It promised shelter in its vastness. And then there was Ruth's sister Marion, who waited at the apartment complex with keys and basic supplies.

"Welcome home," Marion said simply as she lead them to their second-floor unit. The windows faced east, a detail Glenda would later recognize as a gift. It was as though they would always see the sun rising, never setting.

Neither of them could know then that this freedom would be temporary, that the very skills that had helped them escape would eventually trap Michele in darker ways, or that the radiation exposure from those late-night cleaning shifts would return to claim Glenda's life. For now, they stood together in their new apartment as they watched the Montana sunset paint the sky in colors Texas had never shown them.

"Remember this moment, baby," Glenda said softly as she held Michele close. "This is where our new life begins."

Chapter 2:
A Mother's Strength

That first night in Montana set the pattern for their new life. Glenda pushed a dresser against the door, checked the windows three times, and then held Michele until they both slept. Their breathing synchronized in the thin mountain air, each inhale tasting of possibility, each exhale carrying away a bit of Texas terror.

The years that followed their escape were proof of Glenda's determination. The apartment complex, managed by Ruth's sister Marion, became their sanctuary, for it was a place where broken families came to rebuild their lives. Each resident had their own story of flight. They all contributed in some way or the other with their own methods of keeping watch. They formed an unspoken network of survivors, each adding a layer to their collective security.

Their unit was on the second floor, a one-bedroom space with windows that faced east. Every morning, Glenda would wake before sunrise to watch the sky transform, the darkness giving way to brilliant streaks of pink and gold. These quiet moments became her meditation, her time to gather strength for the day ahead.

"Mama, are you making wishes again?" Michele would ask, finding her mother at the window.

"No, baby," Glenda would reply, drawing her daughter close. "I'm counting our blessings." It was Glenda's way of making her daughter feel reassured, providing a shield from the harsh realities of life.

Meanwhile, the blessings she was ever so grateful for — those blessings often came disguised as challenges. Their first winter in Montana tested how capable and strong the mother and daughter were to withstand the harsh winters — of not just the weather but of life as well. The cold was different here, for it was sharp and clean, nothing like the damp Texas chill they'd known. Glenda worked three jobs to keep them afloat. Her jobs comprised morning shifts at the local diner, afternoon cleaning at a motel, and evening bookkeeping for a small automotive shop.

Her hands told the story of their survival. Once soft and manicured—a point of pride in her previous life—they became calloused and raw from constant work. Yet every night, those same hands would gently brush Michele's hair, tie ribbons for school, and tuck her daughter into bed with the tenderness of a woman who knew the value of gentle touch.

The diner where Glenda worked, The Blue Plate Special, became their second home. The owner, Frank Martinez, recognized something in her during the interview. The way she positioned herself to watch the door, how she could recall every customer's movement without seeming to look. He understood what actually was happening from he had his own history of family violence.

"My mama ran with four kids and nothing but change in her pocket," he told Glenda, sliding her application into his desk drawer without looking at it. "Anyone who's got the courage to start over deserves a chance."

He gave her more than a chance—he gave her dignity. Unlike the Texas diner where she'd hidden her tips in Michele's bed frame, here she earned a fair wage and respect from her colleagues. Frank made sure Michele always had a hot meal waiting after school, and his wife Sarah began tutoring her in math when her grades started slipping.

"Your girl's smart as a whip," Sarah would say, watching Michele work through complex problems. "She just needs stability to shine."

Stability was what Glenda worked tirelessly to provide. She created routines that gave Michele's world structure: homework at the diner counter, Saturday morning pancakes, Sunday trips to the library. Each ritual was a brick in the foundation of their new life.

But building that foundation meant sacrificing pieces of herself. Glenda worked through fevers, through exhaustion, through the bone-deep weariness that came from constantly looking over her shoulder. Even in Montana, Harold's shadow lingered. It felt as if he was still watching her every move, every step, lurking in the shadows. Every police siren made her jump, every unexpected knock at the door sent her heart racing.

The library became their Sunday sanctuary, a place where both mother and daughter could dream of different lives. Michele devoured books about far-off places while Glenda studied for her GED in quiet corners between shifts. The elderly librarian, Ms. Abigail, kept a special shelf of holds for them behind the desk.

"Knowledge is power," Ms. Abigail would say, slipping

extra books into their checkout pile. "And nobody can take that away from you."

But knowledge couldn't shield them from all the hardships that were ready to come at them with all their might. The series of hardships began when their first Christmas in Montana brought with it a brutal flu that laid Glenda low for nearly two weeks. She couldn't afford to miss work, so she pushed through shifts with a fever, hiding her coughs behind her apron.

"Mama, you're burning up," Michele said worriedly, pressing a cool washcloth to her mother's forehead late one night.

"I'm fine, baby," Glenda insisted, though her voice was barely a whisper. "Just need to rest a minute."

It was Frank who finally intervened, finding Glenda nearly collapsed in the diner's kitchen. Her skin had taken on a gray pallor he recognized from his own mother's illness years before.

"You're no good to anyone dead," he said gruffly, sending her home with two weeks' paid leave and daily meals delivered by Sarah. But his eyes held a deeper concern as he watched her stumble to Sarah's waiting car.

That illness made it evident that their lives were about to change yet again, making both the mother and daughter navigate through the rough waters of life. The community they'd carefully kept at arm's length rallied around them, helping them, providing them with support in any way they could. Marion reduced their rent temporarily. Regular customers from the diner dropped off medicine and groceries.

Sarah organized a schedule of women to check in on them daily.

For Michele, watching others care for her mother was a revelation. In the blink of an eye, little Michele would find herself in completely different shoes. At nine, she'd grown accustomed to being Glenda's primary support, a role reversal born of trauma. Seeing her mother accept help, albeit reluctantly, gave Michele permission to be a child again.

But healing wasn't going to come easy. And it was certainly not linear. Nightmares plagued them both. Michele would wake screaming, convinced Harold had found them. Glenda's terrors were quieter—she'd jolt awake in cold sweats, checking locks repeatedly through the night.

Their neighbor across the hall, Eleanor, was a retired nurse who recognized the signs of PTSD. She introduced them to breathing exercises and herbal teas, small comforts that helped ease their anxious minds. But she also noticed something else in Glenda's persistent cough, the way she tired too easily, how her weight dropped despite Sarah's hearty diner meals.

"Trauma lives in the body," Eleanor explained one evening, showing Michele how to ground herself during panic attacks. "But so does healing." She left unsaid her growing concern about the other things that might be living in Glenda's body. They showed signs of her having traces of her work at both nuclear plants, accumulating like shadows in her bones.

Glenda threw herself into learning everything she could about trauma recovery. She attended free workshops at the women's center, borrowed psychology books from the library, and joined a support group for domestic violence survivors. Each step forward strengthened her resolve to create a better life for Michele.

The support group became particularly vital to their healing. Every Tuesday evening, while Michele attended youth group at the local church, Glenda sat in a circle of women who understood her fears without explanation.

"I keep waiting for the other shoe to drop," she admitted during one session, voicing a fear she'd never shared with Michele. "He's got eleven more years before possible parole, but sometimes I wake up certain he's found us."

Maria, a fellow survivor with graying hair and kind eyes, reached for her hand. "That fear doesn't go away completely," she acknowledged. "But it gets quieter. You learn to live around it, not because of it."

Work became Glenda's anchor, even as it quietly poisoned her. At the diner, she was known for her quick smile and gentle efficiency. Regular customers requested her section, leaving generous tips and small gifts for Michele. She saved every extra dollar, creating an emergency fund that grew slowly but steadily.

The automotive shop where Glenda did bookkeeping offered her additional training in accounting. Mr. Peterson, the owner, saw potential in her meticulous nature and hunger to learn more. But he also noticed how she struggled to climb the stairs to his office, how her breathing grew labored during long shifts.

"You've got a head for numbers," he told her, helping her

enroll in a community college accounting course. Then, more gently: "And we can move your desk downstairs, near the window. Better air circulation down there."

Glenda studied late into the nights, long after Michele had gone to bed. Her daughter would often find her asleep at their small kitchen table, textbooks, and worksheets scattered around her, a hand pressed against her chest as if to hold something in.

"Why do you work so hard, Mama?" Michele asked one morning, helping to organize the papers.

Glenda looked at her daughter—really looked at her—seeing how she'd grown in their two years in Montana. The constant fear in her eyes had dimmed, replaced by curiosity and hope. But there was still something watchful there, a survivor's instinct that no child should have to develop.

"Because you deserve everything, baby," she answered softly. "And I'm going to make sure you have the chances I never did."

Spring brought change to Montana, the melting snow revealing both new growth and hidden damage. For Glenda, it marked three years since their escape, and with that milestone came a subtle shift in her health. The persistent cough she'd developed during her bout with the flu never fully disappeared. Instead, it deepened, becoming a regular reminder of the toll their new life—and her old one—was taking on her body.

"It's nothing," she insisted whenever Michele expressed concern. "Just the mountain air taking some getting used to."

But Michele noticed other changes, too. Her mother's

once-thick hair began thinning, coming away in strands on her brush. Dark circles appeared beneath her eyes, no matter how many hours she slept. The weight she'd lost during their first winter never returned, leaving her uniform hanging loose on her frame.

At the diner, Sarah started adding extra portions to Glenda's meals, sharing worried glances with Frank whenever she left food untouched. Eleanor began documenting symptoms in her nurse's notebook, comparing them to what she remembered from her years working with radiation-exposure patients.

"You need to see a doctor," Sarah finally said one afternoon, catching Glenda during a quiet moment between shifts. "The free clinic has evening hours—no excuse not to go."

Glenda resisted medical care with the stubbornness that had kept them alive this long. Every spare dollar went into their emergency fund or Michele's future. Doctor visits were a luxury they couldn't afford, especially with Michele growing so fast and needing new clothes every few months.

But their community had other ideas. Eleanor began documenting Glenda's symptoms with professional precision. Mr. Peterson offered to adjust her work schedule to accommodate medical appointments. Even Ms. Abigail contributed, researching medical assistance programs and sliding-scale clinics.

"Sometimes accepting help is the strongest thing you can do," Eleanor reminded her, pressing a handful of clinic paperwork into her hands.

Michele found the papers later that night, hidden beneath her mother's accounting textbooks. The words "possible exposure" and "occupational hazard" jumped out at her, though she didn't fully understand their meaning. What she did understand was the fear she saw in her mother's eyes when she caught her reading them.

"Is it because of the nuclear plant?" Michele asked, remembering the facility where her mother had worked in Texas. "The one near Daddy's station?"

Glenda's face paled. They rarely spoke of the life they had before they came to Montana and never of Harold's workplace. The police station had been just down the road from the power plant where Glenda had worked as a cleaning contractor, exposed to who knew what kind of radiation.

"Some things from our past follow us," Glenda finally answered, pulling Michele close. "But that doesn't mean they get to win."

The first doctor's appointment confirmed their fears while revealing new ones. The exposure at both plants had likely contributed to Glenda's declining health, but stress and overwork had masked the symptoms until they couldn't be ignored.

"We need to run more tests," the doctor explained with her kind but serious face. "There are some concerning masses we need to investigate."

The word "masses" hung in the air like a storm cloud. Michele, waiting in the lobby with Sarah, didn't hear the diagnosis, but she felt its weight in her mother's tight hug afterward.

That night, their small apartment was filled with the sounds of Glenda's muffled crying. Michele lay awake in their shared bedroom, listening to her mother pray—not for herself, but for more time with her daughter.

"Please, God," Glenda whispered into the darkness. "Let me see her grow up. Let me keep her safe long enough to make sure she'll be okay."

Meanwhile, the community mobilized with quiet efficiency. Frank adjusted Glenda's schedule around treatments while Sarah organized a meal train. Eleanor accompanied them to medical appointments, translating medical jargon and advocating for better care.

But no one could prepare them for the legal storm brewing. Harold, learning of Glenda's illness through distant relatives, began filing paperwork for custody rights. His release wasn't for years, but his new wife—barely older than a teenager herself—was deemed a suitable guardian.

"He can't have her," Glenda raged during a lucid moment between treatments, her frail body shaking with fury. "Not after everything. Not my baby." The effort sent her into a coughing fit that left spots of blood on her tissue. Each drop was a reminder of how little time remained.

The court-appointed social worker visited their apartment, taking notes on their living conditions and Michele's care arrangements. Despite the community's testimonies about their stability and support system, the system's gears had begun turning toward what they deemed "the child's best interests."

Mr. Peterson created a new position for Glenda that allowed her to work from home when she wasn't feeling well. "We're computerizing our accounting system anyway," he said gruffly, installing a secondhand computer in their apartment. "Might as well have someone reliable handling it."

The last months of Glenda's life became a desperate race against time. Between treatments that left her weak and nauseous, she focused on preparing Michele for a future she wouldn't be a part of. Every moment together became a lesson, a memory, a final gift from a mother to her daughter.

"Remember to check the locks twice," Glenda would say, her voice growing weaker. "Always keep some emergency money where nobody can find it. Trust your instincts—they'll never steer you wrong."

Michele absorbed everything, understanding too well what these lessons meant. At eleven, she had become her mother's primary caregiver, learning to change IV lines, measure medications, and recognize when pain required immediate attention. The role reversal aged her beyond her years, but she shouldered the responsibility without complaint.

Their evening ritual changed over time. Instead of Glenda reading bedtime stories, Michele would read to her mother, one hand holding the book while the other stroked Glenda's thinning hair. They worked through "Little Women," "Anne of Green Gables," and other stories of strong girls facing adversity. Each story was carefully chosen, carrying messages Glenda hoped would guide Michele after she was gone.

"You're like Jo March," Glenda whispered one night, her

voice barely audible. "Strong, brave, and too smart for your own good sometimes."

The community continued their support, but there was an underlying shift in their attention. It went from helping them build a new life to preparing for its inevitable upheaval. Eleanor started teaching Michele basic nursing skills. Sarah spent hours helping her memorize important phone numbers and addresses. Mr. Peterson set up a small trust fund with Glenda's remaining salary.

In her final weeks, Glenda fought the custody proceedings with whatever strength remained. She documented everything. The list extended to Harold's abuse patterns, his manipulation of law enforcement connections, his history of using official channels for personal vendettas, and every manner he chose to put her through difficulty, making her life a living hell. Each page was both testimony and warning, a map of the dangers Michele would face alone. She had no clue what awaited her the morning to come after.

One crisp autumn morning, Michele woke to find Eleanor in their apartment, tears streaming down her face.

"Your mama loved you more than anything in this world," Eleanor said, gathering Michele into her arms. "She held on as long as she could."

The funeral was small but attended by their entire Montana family. Frank closed the diner for the day, an unprecedented gesture that spoke volumes about Glenda's impact on their lives. Michele stood dry-eyed through the service, clutching Mr. Hoppy—now worn and patched—as person after person shared stories about her mother's courage and kindness.

The legal machine moved with cold efficiency. Within days of Glenda's burial, Michele found herself in an airport, a small suitcase containing the carefully chosen remnants of her life with her mother. The social worker's words blurred together. They were something about fresh starts and family obligations.

Michele's last view of Montana was through tears she'd finally allowed herself to shed. She now had to confront what she thought she and her mother had left behind, never to look back. The mountains that had sheltered them disappeared beneath clouds as the plane carried her back to Texas, back to the source of their nightmares.

Chapter 3:
Descent into Darkness

Harold's new wife met her at the airport. It was all forced smiles and brittle politeness. "You'll learn to love it here," she said, leading Michele to a car that smelled of leather and cigarettes. "Your father's so excited to have you home."

Home — The word felt like ash in Michele's mouth. Home was a small apartment with eastern-facing windows. Home was the smell of Diner's coffee and the sound of her mother's prayers. *That* was what "Home" was for Michele. Alas! That *Home* was gone.

The drive to Harold's place which once was her home, was not an easy one. As they drove through familiar Texas landscapes, Michele clutched her mother's last letter in her pocket, the paper worn soft from constant handling. She found herself unconsciously cataloging details the way Glenda had taught her: monitoring traffic patterns, noting possible escape routes, identifying public places where someone might help. The survival skills her mother had instilled now felt like both armor and prophecy.

The house on Cedar Street looked smaller than she remembered, its manicured lawn and fresh paint a facade as false as Amanda's welcome. Michele stood at the bottom of the driveway, her small suitcase heavy with memories, as her stepmother—barely twenty-two—ushered her toward the front door.

The interior smelled of lemon cleaner and stale cigarettes. Family photos lined the walls. But it was not the family she once had with Glenda and Harold. Rather, the photos were of Harold' and Amanda's wedding, their church gatherings, forced smiles in matching outfits. Michele was a bit unsettled — sad to notice that there were no pictures of her mother, no acknowledgment of the life that existed before. They had erased Glenda as thoroughly as if she had never existed.

"Your father will be home at six," Amanda announced, her voice sharp with artificial sweetness. "Until then, let's go over the rules."

The rules came rapid-fire, each one a new chain: no phone calls without permission, no visitors, no leaving the property without supervision, no closed doors, no complaints, no crying. Michele stood in the entryway, clutching her suitcase, as Harold and Amanda stripped away her remaining freedoms one by one.

Her "bedroom" was a converted storage closet stripped of any personality or comfort. A twin bed and metal desk served as the only furniture. The window, which overlooked the neighbor's brick wall, was nailed shut. "You'll need to earn privileges," Amanda explained, her voice dripping with a sweetness that was laced with something connive, something villainous. "Like curtains. Or a door." The smile that found itself on the lips of Amanda made it evident for Michele that things were going to take a turn for the worse — they had already taken a turn for the worse.

Michele recognized the tactics, for she was very much familiar with them. Isolation, control, surveillance, her mother had taught her to identify these patterns, but knowing the cage doesn't make it easier to escape. She began mapping the house in her mind, just as she had done in Montana, but this time not for comfort. This time, it was for survival.

The first week established the pattern of psychological warfare that would define her captivity. Harold used his security training to implement a system of constant surveillance. Cameras appeared in common areas, motion sensors on windows, alarms on every door. "For your protection," he claimed, though Michele understood they were really for control.

She recognized the irony. The same security measures that had kept her safe in Montana were now being used to imprison her. The habits her mother had taught her became a double-edged sword: checking sight lines, monitoring exits, reading people's moods. These skills kept her alive but reminded her constantly of what she'd lost.

Amanda proved to be an eager participant in Michele's torment. A former victim of abuse herself, she had transformed into an abuser, finding power in causing pain to someone more vulnerable. She took particular pleasure in using food as a weapon, serving Michele meals she was allergic to, then reporting her "defiance" when she couldn't eat.

The bathroom scale became Amanda's favorite instrument of torture. Daily weigh-ins were accompanied by brutal commentary about Michele's body, always with comparisons to her "fat, lazy mother." When Michele's weight dropped below 90 pounds, Amanda celebrated it as "progress."

At night, Michele would press her fingers against her protruding ribs, counting them like prayer beads. The hunger became a kind of comfort—something she could control when everything else was chaos. This relationship with denial and control would later fuel her descent into addiction, though she couldn't know that yet.

Travis, Michele's stepbrother, completed the trinity of torment. Two years older and already showing signs of his father's cruelty, he took special pleasure in psychological abuse. His presence in the house added a new layer of terror to Michele's nights, his footsteps in the hallway enough to send her heart racing.

He would leave "gifts" on Michele's bed—items he claimed to have found in the attic belonging to Glenda. A hairbrush. A faded receipt. Once, horrifyingly, her mother's wedding ring. Each item would disappear before Michele could hide it, proving Travis had access to her room while she slept.

"Want to know what Dad told me about your mom's last days?" he would taunt, dangling Glenda's necklace just out of reach. The implication that Harold had somehow been involved in Glenda's death ate at Michele's psyche, though she never dared ask for clarification.

School offered no respite. Harold had enrolled her in a strict private Christian academy where teachers were informed of her "troubled background." Her previous excellent grades from Montana were dismissed as fraudulent. Every assignment was scrutinized, every interaction monitored for signs of her mother's "corrupting influence."

The isolation was meticulously crafted. Letters to friends in Montana were intercepted and destroyed. Phone calls were monitored, then prohibited entirely. Even her court-mandated therapy sessions became another tool of control—Harold had connections with Dr. Matthews, who used their sessions to reinforce Harold's narrative of Michele's "delusions" about abuse.

"Your mother filled your head with lies," Dr. Matthews would say, his pen scratching notes in a leather-bound notebook. "She created false memories to turn you against your father. But we can help you see the truth."

Michele learned to disappear inside herself during these sessions, finding that quiet place her mother had taught her about. She would retreat there during the worst moments, imagining herself back in the Montana apartment, watching the sunrise with Glenda. This ability to mentally escape, to separate mind from body, would later make it easier to endure the horrors of trafficking—a survival skill that would become both a blessing and a curse.

Physical abuse escalated gradually but systematically. Amanda's slaps became punches, carefully placed where bruises wouldn't show. Harold's "discipline" sessions grew longer and more sadistic, often involving stress positions or sleep deprivation. Travis's nightly visits became more frequent and violent, his father's implicit permission emboldening his actions.

Michele's body began showing the strain. Beyond the weight loss and visible bruises, she developed chronic stomach problems from stress and malnutrition. Her hair started falling out in clumps. Dark circles appeared under her eyes from constant hypervigilance. But any mention of medical care was dismissed.

"You're just attention-seeking," Amanda would snap. "If you'd eat properly and pray more, you wouldn't be sick."

Religion was not lost amongst the tools used to keep her under the clutches. Harold insisted on twice-daily Bible study sessions, using scripture to justify his abuse. "Spare the rod, spoil the child" became his favorite quotation, while his interpretation of "rod" grew increasingly creative and cruel.

To survive, Michele developed elaborate systems of protection. She mapped the house's creaking floorboards, memorized everyone's schedules, created hiding spots so small only she could access them. Behind a loose panel in her closet, she kept her mother's final letter and a small photo of them in Montana, salvaged from Amanda's attempts to erase all evidence of her previous life.

The breaking point began building during her sophomore year. After discovering Michele's hidden journal documenting the abuse, Harold orchestrated a particularly brutal punishment session. For three days, she was locked in the basement storage room—a concrete cell with only a bucket for necessities and no food. Harold called it "reflection time." Michele called it torture.

In the darkness of that basement, Michele retreated deep into herself, finding that quiet place her mother had taught her about. She recited the phone numbers Sarah had made her memorize, whispered the stories her mother had read to her, imagined the smell of Frank's diner coffee. But with each passing hour, those memories felt more distant, like photographs fading in harsh sunlight.

The aftermath of that basement punishment marked a shift in Michele's survival strategy. She learned to say what they wanted to hear, to parrot back their version of reality. It was safer that way. But in her heart, she held onto her mother's truth like a hidden flame, ready to set ablaze the lives of all those who played a part in making hers a living hell.

School performance came no different, there was a role to play there, too. Despite maintaining straight As through sheer determination, every achievement was dismissed as fraud or manipulation. When Michele's English essay about her mother won a state competition, the principal called a meeting with Harold.

"We're concerned about Michele's... imagination," the principal said, sliding the essay across his desk. "These stories she's writing about abuse and salvation. They reflect poorly on the school's values."

The essay was buried, the award rescinded. Michele was transferred out of advanced classes into "special guidance" with Dr. Matthews, who used her writing as evidence of her "persistent delusions." The one outlet she had for processing her pain was systematically stripped away.

The loss of this creative escape drove Michele to find other ways to numb herself. She began experimenting with whatever she could find in the medicine cabinet, learning which combinations of pills could help her float above the pain. This early exploration of chemical escape would later bloom into full addiction, though at the time, it felt like pure survival.

One particularly harrowing night, after a session of Harold's "discipline," Michele found herself contemplating escape. She had carefully mapped the house's vulnerabilities, noted patrol patterns of neighborhood security, even stashed small amounts of food and clothing in various hiding spots.

But escape wasn't simple. Harold's connections in law enforcement meant any attempt would need to be perfect. One failure would mean consequences worse than anything she'd experienced so far. The memory of her mother's careful planning, of the years spent preparing for their flight from Texas, weighed heavily on her mind. Now, all she had to wait was for the right time to execute.

Her opportunity came unexpectedly. During a rare family outing to church, Michele overheard Harold discussing an upcoming business trip. Three days where he would be out of state. Three days where Amanda's vigilance might slip.

The plan formed slowly, carefully. Each detail had to be perfect. Each step meticulous, for there was no room for error. She memorized bus schedules during their weekly grocery trips, stole quarters from Amanda's laundry money, documented security patrol patterns in the neighborhood. Her mother's lessons about escape planning echoed in her mind—never use credit cards, avoid main roads, trust no one with a uniform.

She chose a night when Harold was working a double shift at his security job. Amanda had taken sleeping pills after a particularly vicious argument with Harold. Travis was at a friend's house. The timing would never be better.

Using skills learned from years of enforced silence, Michele gathered her emergency supplies: the hidden photo of her mother, Glenda's letter, a small amount of cash, and Mr. Hoppy, recently discovered in the basement storage room. She changed into layers of clothing, knowing she might not have access to warm clothes for a while.

The window in her room had been nailed shut months ago, but Michele had slowly worked one nail loose, covering her work with a poster of Jesus that Amanda had insisted she display. It took nearly an hour of silent struggle to create an opening wide enough to squeeze through.

The fall from the second floor was terrifying but calculated. Michele had practiced dropping her backpack to test the landing spot, choosing an area where ornamental bushes might break her fall. The impact still drove the air from her lungs and scraped her arms raw, but she forced herself to move.

And just like that, she found herself out of the cage—for how long, nobody could tell. The Texas night was humid, pressing against Michele's skin as she ran through back alleys and drainage ditches. Each streetlight felt like a spotlight, every passing car a potential threat. She had memorized the route to the truck stop during rare family outings, calculating distances and hiding spots with desperate precision.

Her mother's voice echoed in her head: "If you ever have to run, baby, don't take main roads. Stay where people can't see you, but *you* can see them. And remember—truckers help truckers' families."

But Michele never made it to the truck stop. Someone had

spotted her leaving the neighborhood and called it in—another of Harold's endless eyes in the community. Police cruisers converged on her location, Harold's former colleagues eager to prove their loyalty.

They didn't take her home. Instead, they drove to a motel on the outskirts of town, a place where screams wouldn't draw attention. Amanda was waiting in one of the rooms, her face a mask of righteous fury. The officers left with knowing looks— they'd seen enough domestic "discipline" during their years working with Harold to know when to turn a blind eye.

"You ungrateful little whore," Amanda hissed once the door closed. "After everything we've done for you."

What followed was eighteen hours of systematic torture disguised as discipline. They took turns berating her, denying her water, forcing her to stand in stressful positions while reciting Bible verses about honoring thy father. When she collapsed, they simply propped her back up.

Through it all, Michele retreated to that quiet place in her mind where her mother's love still lived. It was the only string helping her to hold on to dear life. She thought of Montana's mountains, of Sarah's cooking, of Frank's gruff kindness. She remembered Eleanor's words about trauma living in the body—but so did strength. This ability to disconnect from her body during trauma would later become both a tool for survival and a curse during her years in trafficking.

The next day, they took her to the sheriff's department. Michele expected more of the same treatment, but something had changed. A deputy she didn't recognize pulled her aside while Harold was filling out paperwork.

"What do you want?" the deputy asked quietly, his eyes kind but serious. "Tell me the truth. What will happen if you go back?"

Michele looked at him, really looked, and saw someone who might actually listen. The words came in a rush, barely above a whisper: "If they take me back, I'll kill them. Or I'll run away for good. Or I'll just end it myself."

Something in her tone must have convinced him. Within twenty-four hours, Child Protective Services launched an emergency investigation. Harold, faced with mounting evidence and the threat of his past crimes being re-examined, made a calculated decision. He terminated his parental rights.

Michele was taken to juvenile detention, placed in solitary confinement for her "own protection." The cell was small, bare, and windowless—but for the first time in months, she felt something close to safe. The silence, once used to torture her, became a blanket of protection.

Her final departure from Harold's house was eerily quiet. Her belongings—what few remained—sat on the porch in a garbage bag while her "family" watched from behind curtains. There were no goodbyes, no words exchanged. As the car pulled away, Michele felt a complex mixture of relief and sorrow. She was free from Harold's grasp, but the scars of her past would follow her forever, etched deep somewhere in her soul.

What she couldn't know then was that this pattern— escape, capture, punishment, rescue—would repeat itself throughout her life. Each cycle would take her deeper into darkness until drugs became her only escape, and her body became currency in a different kind of prison.

The Southern Baptist foster home stood proudly on the Texas plains, shaped like an octagon—a beautiful symbol of Preacher Thomas's dream for harmony and care. However, it was not how Michele saw it. For sixteen-year-old Michele, fresh from the sterile safety of juvenile detention, it represented everything she'd learned to distrust: forced family, mandatory love, and the suffocating weight of others' expectations.

Preacher Thomas and his wife Martha greeted her with practiced smiles and open arms—arms Michele deliberately stepped away from. Their welcome packet included a three-page list of house rules, each one detailed with corresponding Biblical justification. But Michele had learned that rules were just prettied-up chains, and "family" was code for control.

"Structure is God's love made manifest," Preacher Thomas explained during her orientation, his voice carrying the singsong cadence of someone used to having his words accepted without question. "You'll find healing through obedience and the embrace of family."

Michele felt her jaw tighten at the word "family." Glenda had been family. Montana had been family. Everything since then was just another prison with different walls.

"We're all God's children here," Martha added, reaching to touch Michele's shoulder. But it was a gesture Michele had learned to avoid smoothly. "We'll help you learn to trust again."

Trust was just another word that tasted like ash in her mouth. Trust had died with her mother, had been buried under Harold's abuse, had been cremated during that motel room punishment. The system's insistence that she open herself to new bonds felt like another form of violence.

The room they assigned her was sparse but clean, with a window overlooking the dusty Texas landscape. For the first time since juvenile detention, she had a door she could close—though not lock. A twin bed with a handmade quilt, a wooden desk, and a Bible constituted her entire world.

"The quilt was made by all our girls," Martha explained proudly. "Each patch represents a soul saved through our family's love."

Michele looked at the quilt and saw only a map of trapped girls, their pain stitched into neat squares and called redemption. She would sleep on top of it, never under it, refusing to be sewn into their narrative of salvation through submission.

Martha led her through the daily schedule with military precision: Dawn prayers at 5:30 am, breakfast devotionals at 6:00 am, homeschool lessons from 8:00 am to 2:00 pm, afternoon chores until 5:00 pm, evening Bible study at 7:00 pm, lights out at 9:00 pm. Every minute was designed to force interaction, to manufacture intimacy through proximity.

"Family meals are mandatory," Martha emphasized, tapping the schedule. "It's where we share our hearts with each other."

Michele had learned from Harold that forced sharing was just another form of surveillance. She ate mechanically, eyes down, volunteering nothing. When pressed to participate in "family discussions," she gave answers so bland they were forgotten before they finished leaving her lips.

"Your file suggests a concerning lack of attachment," Martha noted during one mandatory counseling session, flipping through the thick folder that contained Michele's history. "Your mother's... choices... left you vulnerable to isolation. We need to help you learn to bond properly."

The mention of her mother made Michele's hands clench under the table, but her face remained carefully blank. They could force her to sit here, force her to eat their food, force her to listen to their prayers, but they couldn't force her to give them what they really wanted—her trust, her pain, her inner self. Those belonged to her alone.

James, a fourteen-year-old boy, and Rebecca almost twelve, were the other foster children with Michele. They watched Michele with a mixture of curiosity and wariness. They had the look of true believers—too well-trained to question, too desperate for love to resist the system's demands for emotional submission.

"Just play along," James whispered during chores. "It's easier if they think you're changing."

But Michele had learned from Harold that playing along was how they trapped you, how they made you complicit in your own imprisonment. She refused to participate in the forced hugs, the performative prayers, the tearful confessions during Bible study. Her resistance made her a problem, a challenge to be broken.

Her first taste of chemical escape came unexpectedly. During one of Martha's mandatory "healing sessions," Rebecca showed her where the real medicine cabinet was hidden. It was behind a false panel in the bathroom. "They save the good stuff for themselves," she explained, pointing to prescription bottles with various labels. "Says we need to pray our pain away instead."

Michele recognized some of the bottle labels. Those labels were of the medications her mother had taken during her illness. But where those pills had meant pain and loss, now they represented something different: freedom. The first time she stole a Valium, it wasn't about getting high—it was about finding a way to endure their endless demands for emotional intimacy without actually giving them access to her soul.

The theft became a ritual of resistance. Michele developed a habit without even knowing that she was making one. It was of theft and consumption, learning which medications did what, how to combine them for maximum emotional distance. The hollow cross pendant Martha had given her felt nothing more than another attempt at forced spiritual connection. Michele, in a sense of defiance and rebellion transformed it into the—became the perfect hiding spot for pills. The irony wasn't lost on her.

There were mandatory "Family Sharing" sessions that she could not avoid. However, there was one thing she could really do to get by. So during those unavoidable sessions, the pills helped her maintain the perfect mask of polite disconnection. She could sit through their inquisitive questions, their demands for emotional vulnerability, their constant pressure to "open her heart to healing," while remaining safely fortified behind chemical walls.

"We're seeing progress," Preacher Thomas would note,

mistaking her chemical calm for acceptance. "The Lord is softening her heart."

But Michele wasn't softening. It was far beyond the imagination of the Preacher, for all she was perfecting under the mask of the quiet persona was her act of disappearing. The medications didn't just dull pain. They provided an escape from the suffocating weight of their enforced intimacy, from the constant pressure to perform gratitude for their "salvation."

A trade was coming her way of which she wasn't aware. James caught her one night, stepping silently into her room after lights out. Instead of threatening to tell, he offered a trade: some of her pills for his knowledge of where Preacher Thomas kept the communion wine.

"Sometimes chemicals are better than Christ," he said with a wisdom too old for his years. "At least they don't demand you love them back."

And there it was, the beginning of something. From there began the secret communion. Pills and stolen wine creating a floating sensation that almost felt like peace. And the best part — it was not the false peace they preached about during services, but real freedom from their constant emotional demands.

Rebecca joined their clandestine gatherings, bringing her own contributions—marijuana stolen from Martha's "migraine management" stash, prescription cough syrup from the locked cabinet in the kitchen. Together, they created their own trinity of chemical salvation, a dark mirror of the family bonds their keepers tried so desperately to forge.

"This is real family," Rebecca whispered during one of

their sessions. "No one trying to fix anyone else."

But Michele kept even these conspirators at arm's length. She shared her drugs but never her stories, her space but never her truth. The lessons taught by Harold were now taking the front seat, weaving another web of protection. For he taught her that intimacy was just prelude to betrayal.

Nonetheless, the space that Michele had created for her, stealing pills and allowing James and Rebecca to be accomplices was about to turn into a cloud — a distant, unreachable one. The façade now had to come crumbling down. It began cracking three months into Michele's stay. During a particularly intense "prayer counseling" session, Preacher Thomas found her mother's hidden photo—the last one taken in Montana, showing Glenda and Michele smiling in front of the diner. He saw it not as the precious memory it was, but as evidence of Michele's "unhealthy attachment" to her past.

"This resistance to your new family stems from idolizing your mother," he declared, holding the photo like it was contaminated. "True healing requires letting go of worldly attachments."

When he tore the photo in half, something broke inside Michele. That night, she took twice her usual combination of pills and wine, seeking not just escape but oblivion. The resulting blackout led to her first real act of rebellion—she broke into Preacher Thomas's office and destroyed his prized Bible collection, shredding pages and using communion wine to paint "LIAR" across the walls.

She didn't target just any pages. With methodical precision, she destroyed every passage about honoring thy father, about women's submission, about the sanctity of family. Each shredded verse was a rejection of their demands for emotional surrender, their insistence that healing meant letting others in.

The punishment was severe but came with an unexpected consequence. Word got around to other foster kids in the system about the girl who'd defaced the holy books. Michele's reputation shifted from quiet victim to something more dangerous—someone who refused to break, who rejected not just authority but the very foundation of their enforced family structure.

Tommy, a seventeen-year-old who lived two farms over, started hanging around the property's edge during Michele's outdoor chores. He recognized something in her eyes. It was not just the hollow look of trauma but the fierce refusal to let anyone close.

"I can get you better stuff," he offered one day, showing her a small bag of white powder. "Real freedom, not that prescription bullshit. No one can make you feel anything when you're flying this high."

Methamphetamine entered her life like a lightning bolt, burning away the last threads of her former self. The first hit, taken in Tommy's basement while his parents were at church, felt like touching divinity—if divinity was made of fire and electricity.

"This is living," Tommy whispered, teaching her how to

crush and snort the crystalline powder. "This is power. No one can make you love them when you're like this."

The power came with a price, but Michele had learned from Harold that she deserved nothing better. If she was going to be worthless, she might as well excel at it. The same perfectionism that had once earned her straight As in Montana now drove her deeper into chemical expertise.

"You're a natural," Tommy commented, watching her calculate dosages and combinations with mathematical precision. "Most people just use. You study it."

She did study it, with the same intensity she'd once applied to her mother's escape plans. She learned everything about the drugs she took—chemical compositions, interaction effects, optimal timing. If she was going to destroy herself, she would do it with excellence. No halfway measures, no amateur mistakes.

When she turned seventeen, Michele filed for emancipation. The foster system, eager to be rid of a "problem child," fast-tracked her paperwork. With Tommy's connections, she rented a small house on the outskirts of town. Little did anyone know that it was a place that quickly became a hub for users and dealers.

The house operated on strict rules—no violence inside, no stealing from each other, no dealing to kids. These principles, learned from years of surviving systematic abuse, helped her maintain control over an increasingly chaotic situation. She ran her operation with the same meticulous attention to detail that Glenda had once used to manage their escape fund, but now those skills served her self-destruction.

"You're wasting your potential," one of her regular customers, a former teacher, told her. The comment made her laugh—bitter and hollow.

"This is my potential," she replied, measuring out another line with surgical precision. "Being the best at being the worst."

Her reputation grew. Other dealers noticed how she never miscounted, never missed a payment, never lost control of her territory. She kept immaculate records, ran her business with corporate efficiency, and maintained a facade of functionality that kept police attention at bay. Even in free fall, she remained a perfectionist.

The meth had taken hold of her life with barbed hooks, requiring ever-increasing doses to maintain the same escape. She dropped to 95 pounds, her skin breaking out in sores that she covered with long sleeves and makeup. The mirror became an enemy, reflecting a ghost of who she used to be, but the meth made it possible not to care.

"You're killing yourself," James said during a rare visit, his own addiction showing in his hollow eyes.

"That's the point," she answered, measuring out his dose with the same precision she used for everyone else. "Might as well be the best at that, too."

It was during this calculated descent that she met Johnny. He wasn't like the other dealers—he wore expensive clothes, drove a clean car, and spoke with an education that set him apart from Rick's crude business style. But what really caught his attention was Michele's systematic approach to destruction.

"You run this place like a Fortune 500 company," he

observed during their first meeting, studying her meticulously kept ledgers. "Most tweakers can't even remember what day it is. You've got spreadsheets."

Michele recognized the predatory interest in his gaze, but it didn't matter. Nothing mattered except maintaining her perfect record of imperfection. When he offered to show her "how to turn this into a real business," she heard the trap in his words and walked into it anyway.

"You're wasting your potential here," Johnny said, silently assessing her makeshift operation with calculated interest. "I can show you how to be the best. No more amateur hour." For in his eyes, the girl really did have it in her — it was natural.

And then there was the word that he'd used for her. The word "best" hooked her more than any drug could. If she was going to sell her soul, why not to the highest bidder? Johnny's world seemed glamorous compared to her current situation. He introduced her to higher-level suppliers, taught her about cutting and processing meth, showed her how to maximize profits through careful distribution. That meant something.

What she didn't realize was that each lesson came with invisible chains. Each lesson that came, was like a nail in the coffin but not the final one, for the final nail was not due just yet. Meanwhile, Johnny was grooming her, creating dependencies that went beyond mere addiction. He started managing her money, controlling her supply, deciding who she could sell to. The control was so gradual she barely noticed until it was complete.

Chapter 4:
Chemical Chains

The first time Johnny injected her, he called it a sign of trust. "Only family shares needles," he explained, tying off her arm with practiced efficiency that spoke of countless victims before her. The word "family" should have raised red flags for Michele—it had always brought her pain rather than comfort. Yet, in that moment, the euphoria flooded in, overshadowing any caution she felt. By the time she began to grasp the true cost of her choices, she found herself ensnared in a complex web of control that would take years of struggle to break free from.

Johnny's sprawling ranch-style house became Michele's new prison, where chemical and physical restraints merged into a calculated blueprint of captivity. Each room became a psychological experiment in submission. The security cameras weren't just for surveillance—they were constant reminders that every moment of vulnerability, every private breakdown, every silent tear was being watched and recorded. The feeling of being perpetually observed slowly eroded her sense of self until she began to see herself through their eyes: as property, as inventory, as a thing to be managed.

The blue room, her designated space near Johnny's quarters, embodied the cruel duality of her captivity. It offered the illusion of personal space while serving as another layer of control. The walls, painted a calm shade of blue meant to suggest serenity, seemed to close in tighter with each passing day. Each night, she would carefully feel for the concealed anchors for restraints nestled behind the elegant panels. It struck her that even the decor was crafted to reinforce her role—every exquisite detail in the house seemed to carry a sharp edge.

"Can't have my best girl running off," Johnny would say while fastening the cuffs, his voice gentle but his eyes calculating. "You're too valuable to lose." The word 'valuable' became a psychological anchor, twisting her own sense of worth into something that only existed in relation to her usefulness to him. She began to measure her own humanity in dollar signs and decimals, her identity dissolving into spreadsheet cells and profit margins.

The injection ritual evolved into an elaborate ceremony of mental dominance. Johnny understood that breaking someone wasn't just about physical control—it was about replacing their reality with your own. He created a perverse family structure among his "favorites," forcing them to participate in each other's degradation. Clean needles became rewards for betraying confidences, reporting escape plans, identifying weaknesses in others that could be exploited. The guilt of survival became another chain, heavier than any steel restraint.

It did not stop there, though, for the injection ritual became increasingly elaborate. Johnny would gather his "favorites" in the main room, creating a perverse ceremony out of their dependence. In order to get your hands on clean needles, you had to pay a price. Nevertheless, the price came at the cost of not the one reporting, but the one being reported. It became a privilege — the one that was to be earned through compliance. Resistance meant being given used ones, with all the risks that entailed.

"You're my best girl," he'd whisper while tying off her arm, his gentle tone masking the violence of the act. "So smart, so reliable. Just need to keep you focused."

The focus came at a terrible price. The cocktail of drugs he used—meth cut with heroin, laced with whatever else he was experimenting with—kept them compliant but conscious. Michele's body began breaking down under the constant assault. Her veins collapsed one by one, forcing Johnny to find new injection sites. She developed abscesses that he treated with crude home remedies, refusing to risk hospital visits.

Physical restraints were just one piece of the control puzzle. Security cameras kept a watchful eye on every corner of the facility. Daily changing door codes added an extra layer of security. Guards, often individuals trapped by their own addictions, roamed the grounds as part of their debt repayment. However, the true shackles were chemical in nature. Johnny's unique concoction made withdrawal not just painful, but potentially fatal, if he didn't step in to intervene.

Michele's life was marked by constant violence. She was beaten by dealers, assaulted by customers, and threatened by the men who claimed to protect her. One night, Johnny set her up to fail, orchestrating a deal that left her owing him for stolen drugs. When she couldn't pay, he put a hit on her life. At work, she was cornered by four men and thrown across a pool table. They demanded money and drugs, threatening to kill her if she didn't comply. A bouncer's intervention saved her, but the escape was temporary.

Her final night in Texas was a narrow escape. Trapped in a fast-food drive-thru, two cars pinned her in. Men armed with guns stepped out, ready to finish what they had started. In a moment of sheer desperation, Michele floored the gas pedal, ramming the car in front of her and jumping a curb. Gunfire shattered her rear window as she sped away, bullets missing her by inches. Her heart pounding and mind racing, she drove north through the night, her body running on pure adrenaline and whatever chemicals still coursed through her system. At barely 95 pounds, weak from starvation and exhaustion, she pushed on until the Texas border disappeared in her rearview mirror.

Michele's intelligence, once her armor against the world, became another weapon in her own destruction. Johnny recognized her drive for excellence and weaponized it, making her complicit in her own captivity. She became his perfect project—the addict who could still do complex mathematics, the prisoner who maintained his elaborate books, the broken girl who could break others with efficient precision. Each successful calculation, each balanced book, and each new girl processed into the system became another brick in the wall between her past self and what she was becoming.

The psychological impact of managing her own exploitation created fractures in her identity. During the day, she would record transactions with professional detachment, treating her own body as just another asset to be logged and depreciated. At night, she would dissociate into complex mathematical equations, finding a kind of escape in the cold clarity of numbers. The part of her that still remembered being human would retreat deeper with each entry, every column of figures becoming another layer of emotional scar tissue.

Her body's breakdown under the constant chemical assault mirrored her psychological deterioration. As her veins collapsed one by one, forcing Johnny to find increasingly creative injection sites, she felt pieces of her identity collapsing as well. The abscesses he treated with crude home remedies left both physical and emotional scars—permanent reminders that her body, like her mind, was no longer her own. The infections became metaphors for her spreading sense of worthlessness, each new wound confirming what they had taught her: she was damaged goods, useful only as long as she could function through the pain.

The trafficking ring's chillingly organized approach turned Michele's world into a nightmare of psychological torment. She found herself knee-deep in intricate spreadsheets, meticulously monitoring "inventory" and profits while grappling with the harsh reality of reducing the suffering of other women to cold, hard data. She recorded her own degradation in precise decimal points, calculating the exact dollar value of human suffering. The mathematics of exploitation became her expertise—how many girls could be moved through a location before attracting attention, how much product could be pushed before overdoses became statistically problematic, how to balance maximum profit against minimum visibility. Each calculation pulled her further from her humanity, turning her into an unwilling architect of other women's destruction.

Violence served as both punishment and psychological conditioning. Michele endured beatings from dealers, assaults from customers, and calculated abuse from the men claiming to protect her. But the physical pain was almost welcome compared to the psychological torture of being forced to facilitate the abuse of others. Johnny would make her watch as new girls were broken in, knowing that her visible compliance would help convince them to submit. "Show them how to survive," he'd command, turning her survival skills into tools of recruitment.

With no place to turn and no one to reach out to—thanks to Johnny's tight grip on her life—she felt utterly lost. Yet, during a brief moment of solace at the club, a fellow dancer, also seeking to break free from Johnny's clutches, leaned in and shared a glimmer of hope: there were connections waiting for her in Oklahoma. "There are people who can help," she'd said, her eyes darting nervously around the dressing room. "People who know how to disappear girls like us."

Michele almost laughed at that now. She'd already disappeared once with her mother, and look how that turned out. But with bullets in her chest and Johnny's hunters behind her, she didn't have the luxury of better options.

The "help" in Oklahoma revealed itself as another carefully laid trap. Her friend's connections were just another network of predators, more sophisticated in their methods but no less brutal in their intent. They saw her bullet wounds as a brand of ownership—damaged goods they could exploit without consequence. The same men who fixed her up and gave her antibiotics would later use those same wounds to keep her under control.

In Oklahoma, the psychological manipulation escalated to

unprecedented levels. Her new captors improved upon Johnny's techniques, approaching them with a more scientific mindset and treating her as a subject in their control experiments. They tracked her responses to different drug combinations in detailed logs, discussing her reactions with scientific detachment. The dehumanization was complete— she wasn't even property anymore, just data to be analyzed.

They kept her wounds from healing properly, using pain and infection as psychological leverage. When she showed signs of resistance or clarity, they'd press on her injuries until she begged for relief, then administer drugs cut with industrial chemicals. The message was clear: her body, like her mind, belonged to them to break as they pleased. Even her pain wasn't her own—it was just another tool in their arsenal of control.

The high-end parties where they trafficked her became exercises in psychological fragmentation. As she sat quietly in the corner, she couldn't help but watch the wealthy men around her, confidently paying exorbitant prices for the company of women. Their lighthearted conversations drifted toward business deals and lavish family vacations, their laughter echoing in stark contrast to the reality unfolding before her eyes. It was a world where exploitation masked itself in charm and charisma, a façade so polished that it almost felt normal. Her skill with numbers made her valuable for more than just her body—they had her managing their books between "appointments," forcing her to catalog her own violations in precise accounting terms.

The night everything changed started like any other, at

one of these exclusive gatherings in a sprawling mansion on the outskirts of Oklahoma City. Amidst the swirling fog of chemicals, Michele's eyes sharpened as familiar faces from her Texas past came into focus—men who were deeply connected to Johnny's web of dealings. Each one stirred memories long buried, reigniting a spark of recognition that sent a shiver through her. Her captors were negotiating with them, discussing her fate as casually as traders might discuss commodity futures. The bounty on her head had followed her across state lines, and now her past and present collided with devastating force.

What ensued was a grueling eighteen hours of relentless torment that would change Michele's life forever. She was moved from one location to another, with each new environment unveiling a new layer of terror. The violence escalated beyond anything she'd previously endured as multiple groups of men took turns asserting their ownership of her body. Time became fluid, reality fragmenting into sharp pieces of consciousness between blackouts.

The final act of violence came in an abandoned lot on the outskirts of town. Two gunshots to the chest—not meant to kill quickly, but to send a message. As Michele lay bleeding on the cold ground, her mother's words echoed through her fading consciousness: "Sometimes, baby, you have to die to be reborn."

The harsh fluorescent lights of the emergency room would come next, marking the beginning of a different kind of survival story. But in that moment, as life drained from her body onto the frozen earth, Michele experienced a clarity that had eluded her throughout years of addiction and exploitation. Death wasn't just approaching—it was offering a chance at resurrection.

Time splintered into fragments. Moments of awareness broke through in sudden jags: the piercing sound of sirens drawing near, the firm grip of paramedics as they tore away the remnants of her clothing, and chaotic voices calling out numbers and medical jargon that swirled around her, incomprehensible to her fogged thoughts. The ambulance's motion sent waves of agony through her bullet-riddled chest, each bump in the road a fresh reminder that she was, somehow, still alive.

"Female, early twenties, multiple GSWs to the chest," a distant voice called out. "BP dropping, probable pneumothorax, track marks indicating long-term IV drug use." The clinical assessment of her broken body felt like a final bookkeeping entry—one last ledger to balance before the end.

Through it all, Michele clung to the memory of her mother's voice, stronger now than it had been in years. The chemicals that had kept her numb for so long were fading, stripped away by the shock of trauma, leaving her raw and present in her dying body. As her consciousness started to slip away, she spotted her mother in the distant corner of the trauma bay, looking just as she did during their cherished days in Montana.

The emergency room erupted in controlled chaos as they rolled her in. The fluorescent lights above seemed to pulse with her fading heartbeat, each flash illuminating a different face hovering over her. They worked with mechanical efficiency to stabilize her failing body, their urgent voices creating a symphony of medical jargon that washed over her like waves.

"Starting chest tube."

"Push another unit."

"We're losing her."

"Starting compressions."

The pain began to recede, replaced by a floating sensation that should have terrified her but instead felt like a release. Michele had spent years learning to disappear inside herself. It seemed fitting that her final disappearing act would be the most complete.

As her awareness began to fade, she caught a glimpse of her mother in the far corner of the trauma bay, appearing just as she remembered from their days in Montana. Glenda's presence felt more real than the doctors fighting to save her life, more solid than the machines tracking her failing vital signs.

"Hold on, baby," her mother's voice whispered. "This isn't the end of your story."

The darkness took her then, but it wasn't the chemical darkness she'd grown accustomed to. This felt deeper and cleaner somehow, like the black velvet of a Montana night sky. The last sound she registered was the flatline tone of a heart monitor, its singular note marking the boundary between who she had been and who she might become.

Chapter 5:
Resurrection

The first thing Michele became aware of was the steady beeping of monitors, each electronic pulse marking time in a world she hadn't meant to return to. The second was pain. It was not the familiar burn of chemicals in her veins or the ache of abuse but something deeper and more fundamental. It was the pain of being forcibly dragged back into a body she'd tried so desperately to leave behind.

"Welcome back," a nurse said softly, noticing her fluttering eyelids. "You've been with us for three days. Try not to move. You've got some serious repairs holding you together."

She could not help but notice the difference — the stark contrast the ICU room was to the spaces she'd occupied for the past years. Everything was white, sterile, monitored. No hidden cameras, no underlying or concealed meanings, and no price tags attached to human contact. The restraints on her wrists were medical rather than punitive, designed to prevent her from disturbing the maze of tubes and wires keeping her alive.

Detective Sarah Martinez had been waiting for this moment. She stood in the doorway. Her badge caught the fluorescent light much like Harold's used to, but her eyes held something different. It was not authority, no. It was something different than that. It was nothing but recognition. She'd been sitting with Michele's unconscious form for days, reading through the thick file that documented her history. The escape with Glenda, Harold's abuse, the foster home, Johnny's trafficking operation, and finally, the brutal attack that had brought her here was all right in front of the detective's eyes. It was all there in those documents.

It was in the air. Or perhaps Matinez knew for a fact that when Michele would wake up, she'd need to feel safe in order to open up. "You're safe now," Martinez said, pulling a chair close to the bed. "And you're not the first girl they've tried to silence this way. We've been building a case against this network for years. You're not alone anymore."

The words should have meant something, but Michele had heard too many promises of safety, had been "rescued" too many times only to find herself in deeper hells. She turned her face away, retreating into the familiar numbness that had protected her for so long.

But withdrawal had stripped away her chemical armor. Without the drugs to dull her senses, every emotion she'd suppressed came crashing through. The pain wasn't just physical anymore. All feelings pertaining to the years of trauma demanded to be felt, all at once.

"Your body is going through several kinds of withdrawal," Dr. Chen explained during morning rounds. "The bullets did a lot of damage, but the long-term effects of the chemicals in your system..." She trailed off, studying the toxicology reports with a mixture of professional concern and personal horror.

The detox was brutal. Michele's body, already weakened by bullets and years of abuse, rebelled against sobriety. She cycled through fever dreams where Johnny's voice mingled with Harold's, where Amanda's taunts echoed through the foster home's halls, where her mother's last words in Montana became twisted into accusations.

Through it all, a team of trauma specialists worked to keep her alive—not just physically but psychologically. They recognized that her survival depended on more than just healing bullet wounds. They had to help her find a reason to stay in a body that had known nothing but pain for so long.

Eleanor, a psychiatric nurse with gray hair and kind eyes, became her anchor to reality. She would sit with Michele during the worst of the withdrawal, telling stories about other survivors who had rebuilt their lives. "The body remembers everything," she would say, "but it also knows how to heal."

The healing came in unexpected ways. Physical therapy forced Michele to reconnect with her body not as a commodity to be sold, but as something that belonged to her alone. Each small movement was an act of reclamation, each step a declaration of ownership over her own flesh.

Detective Martinez brought an unexpected gift during her third week of recovery. It was a worn stuffed rabbit found in evidence from the shooting scene. Mr. Hoppy, somehow preserved through years of horror, still carried the careful stitches from Michele's childhood attempts to repair him after Harold's rage.

"Your mother documented everything," Martinez explained, placing a thick folder on Michele's lap. "Every abuse, every threat, every connection in Harold's network. She knew someday it might be needed. The information she gathered... it's helping us unravel trafficking operations across three states."

The revelation cracked something open in Michele's chest. All those years, she'd carried her mother's memory like a hidden flame, never knowing that Glenda had left her more than just survival skills. She had left her a weapon against the darkness that had claimed them both.

As her body slowly healed, Michele began working with investigators. Her perfect memory for numbers and transactions served as a different kind of ledger. The same skills that had made her valuable to Johnny now helped dismantle his empire. Each name she provided, each connection she revealed, became an act of resurrection. Her trauma now began to become her weapon.

Did she think healing would come that easily? There were still many bumps in the road to recovery. There was a lot that she still had to face. There were nightmares that plagued her for several months and not just days. Those nightmares were filled with horrors beyond imagination. The sounds of boots on hardwood floors would make her jump in her sleep. The sharp scent of antiseptic felt very much alive even when she drifted off to sleep. During group therapy sessions at the hospital's trauma unit, she struggled to voice her experiences, the words sticking in her throat like shards of glass.

"Recovery isn't about forgetting," Dr. Sarah Williams, her trauma therapist, explained. "It's about remembering in a way that doesn't destroy you. Your story is part of you, but it's not all of you."

However, ther breakthrough wasn't delayed and came unexpectedly. During a particularly difficult physical therapy session, Michele caught her reflection in the hospital window.

The rising sun painted the sky in shades of pink and gold, just like the Montana mornings she'd shared with her mother. For the first time since Glenda's death, she allowed herself to really look at her own face—no longer seeing inventory to be valued, but her mother's daughter, somehow still alive.

"I want to testify," she told Detective Martinez that afternoon. "Not just provide evidence. I want to face them in court. I want them to see that they failed to silence me."

The decision to testify set off a new kind of war. This time the war was rather legal than physical. But she was not going to have an easy fight. Johnny's network had deep connections and deeper pockets. Threats began arriving at the hospital, each one carefully worded to trigger Michele's trauma responses. But this time, she wasn't facing them alone.

A team of survivors' advocates worked to prepare her for court, teaching her how to ground herself when flashbacks threatened to overwhelm her. They helped her understand that her perfect memory, once used to track her own exploitation, could now serve justice.

"Your precision with details, your ability to remember transactions and connections aren't something to be afraid or ashamed of," her court advocate explained. "They aren't wounds. They're tools. You survived by paying attention. Now that attention will help protect others."

A day would come when she would walk on her feet, stronger than ever and that day did not take long to arrive. The day Michele left the hospital, three months after bullets had tried to end her story, she walked out under her own power.

She was not abandoned and Detective Martinez accompanied her to a safe house, where other survivors of trafficking were rebuilding their lives. The building had windows that faced east, and Michele found herself drawn to the sunrise. It was just as though her mother had been in Montana.

"Your mother's case files helped us identify over thirty girls in active trafficking situations," Martinez shared as they watched the sun rise. "Even after death, she's still saving lives. Through you, she's still fighting."

Michele touched the scars on her chest, feeling the steady rhythm of her resurrected heart. She thought of all the ledgers she'd kept over the years, all the calculations of human suffering she'd been forced to record. Now she had a new kind of accounting to do. It was the one that would balance the scales of justice, one testimony at a time.

The sun cleared the horizon, painting the sky in colors of rebirth. Michele remembered her mother's last words in her fever dreams. "Sometimes, baby, you have to die to be reborn." Standing in the dawn light, feeling the weight of Mr. Hoppy in her arms and the truth of her testimony in her heart, Michele finally understood what her mother had meant.

This wasn't just survival anymore. This was resurrection.

The courthouse seemed like a modernist fortress, all glass and steel reaching toward an indifferent sky. Michele stood at the base of its steps, wearing a charcoal suit that Detective Martinez had helped her choose—professional armor for the battle ahead. At 103 pounds, her body still bore the visible marks of her ordeal, but her eyes held something new: purpose.

"Remember," Dr. Williams had told her during their final preparation session, "they'll try to use your precision against you. They'll say your memory can't be trusted because of the drugs. But your attention to detail wasn't because of the chemicals—it was how you survived them."

The defense attorneys had already tried to paint her as an unreliable witness. They cited her history of addiction, her involvement in bookkeeping for the operation, her previous "relationships" with the defendants. Each attempt to discredit her felt like another kind of violation, but Michele had learned to use their attacks as fuel.

Michele stepped into the witness box, feeling the weight of Mr. Hoppy in her bag—a silent testament to every version of herself that had survived to reach this moment. Her voice, when it came, carried the strength of mountains.

"State your name for the record."

"Michele Claire Anderson."

The questioning began gently enough, establishing her history. But as she began detailing the trafficking operation's structure, the defense attorneys grew aggressive. They objected to her methodical recitation of dates, amounts, locations—trying to block the very evidence that would condemn their clients.

"How can you be so certain of these numbers?" they demanded, their tone suggesting impossibility.

Michele's response cut through their attempts at intimidation. "Because I had to balance those books with a gun to my head. Because every mistake meant someone would be hurt or killed. Because I was trained to track human suffering in decimal points, and those numbers were carved into my soul."

Her testimony spanned five days. She documented every transaction, every act of violence, every connection in their network. The same mental vault that had protected her from breaking now opened to reveal its contents with devastating clarity. When they showed her ledgers as evidence, she corrected errors in the prosecution's calculations without referencing notes—showing the jury just how intimate her knowledge of the operation had been.

Johnny sat at the defense table, his expensive suit a poor disguise for what Michele now saw clearly as mundane evil. He tried to catch her eye, to invoke the old power he'd held over her. But Michele kept her gaze steady, letting him see that his psychological holds had no more purchase on her resurrected self.

The most difficult moment came when they played the surveillance footage from the night of her shooting. Michele watched her past self being dragged across the screen and heard the echoes of her own screams. But instead of dissociating, she stayed present—naming each person visible in the grainy footage, providing context for every moment of horror.

"The defendant appears to be smiling in this frame," the prosecutor noted, freezing the video on Johnny's face.

"He always smiled when he thought he was teaching someone a lesson," Michele replied, her voice steady. "He said it was important to enjoy your work."

The jury's shock was palpable, but Michele continued. She detailed how trafficking operations hid behind legitimate businesses, how they groomed vulnerable girls, how they used addiction and violence to maintain control. Her testimony provided a roadmap of exploitation that stretched across multiple states.

When they questioned her about Harold, about her mother, about every trauma that had led her to Johnny's web, Michele didn't flinch. She laid out the pattern of abuse and authority that had made her vulnerable to trafficking, helping the jury understand that her story was just one thread in a larger tapestry of systematic exploitation.

The defense's cross-examination focused on trying to break her precision, to find inconsistencies in her account. But Michele's answers remained measured, exact. When they tried to suggest she had been a willing participant, she turned their questions back on them with devastating clarity.

"Yes, I kept their books," she acknowledged. "I recorded every girl they broke, every dollar they made from human suffering. And now I'm using that same ledger to make them pay for what they did."

The trial lasted three weeks. Michele's testimony became the foundation for multiple convictions, not just of Johnny and his immediate circle, but of dozens of connected traffickers, corrupt officials, and enablers. Her perfect memory for numbers helped prosecutors trace money laundering operations, leading to the seizure of millions in criminal assets.

The day the verdicts were read, Michele sat in the courtroom surrounded by other survivors—women who had found their voices because she had refused to be silenced. Johnny's face turned ashen as the judge read out his sentence: life without possibility of parole. Each additional defendant received similar terms, their combined sentences stretching into centuries.

But it was the civil penalization that struck the deepest blow. The courts seized properties, froze accounts, and dismantled the infrastructure of exploitation. Michele watched as the same accounting skills that had once tracked her own violation now helped redirect millions toward survivor support services.

Outside the courthouse, after the verdicts, Detective Martinez handed Michele a final piece of evidence: Glenda's complete case file, no longer needed for prosecution.

"Your mother never stopped fighting," Martinez said softly. "Everything she documented, every connection she traced while cleaning those offices at night—it was all building toward this moment. She knew someday someone would need this information to break their power."

Michele's hands trembled as she made an attempt to open the file her mom had left her. She could not help but feel amazed seeing her mother's careful handwriting documenting Harold's connections, the trafficking networks that operated under police protection, and the web of corruption that had seemed unbreakable. Glenda had been building a case even as cancer consumed her, ensuring that her daughter would have weapons for the war she knew was coming.

That night, in her small apartment in the survivor housing complex, Michele began a new kind of accounting. She spread her mother's files across the floor alongside the trial transcripts and her own carefully articulated notes. There she saw, a pattern emerging. It was the one that pointed to larger networks, to trafficking operations that extended beyond Johnny's organization.

The sunrise found her still working. Mr. Hoppy propped against her laptop as she cross-referenced data points. Her body ached from sitting on the floor, the bullet scars pulling tight across her chest, but her mind felt clearer than it had in years. She wasn't just surviving anymore, and she wasn't just testifying about her own trauma. She was continuing her mother's work, using their shared skills of observation and precision to expose what others wanted hidden.

Detective Martinez's words from the hospital came back to her. *Even after death, she's still saving lives. Through you, she's still fighting.*

Michele touched the worn fur of Mr. Hoppy's ear, thinking of all the versions of herself that had carried him. Those versions including the terrified child in Harold's house, the girl who fled to Montana, the addict in Johnny's web, the survivor who testified. Each incarnation had protected some small piece of her truth, waiting for the moment when she could finally use it as more than just a shield.

The morning light painted her eastern windows in familiar Montana colors as Michele opened a new spreadsheet. She had ledgers to balance, networks to expose, and a legacy to fulfill. Her mother had died protecting her and had left her the tools to fight back. Now, it was her turn to protect others, to help them find their way back from the dark.

Chapter 6:
A Journey of Transformation

This marked the beginning of Michele's transformation from survivor to advocate. But the path ahead would test her newfound purpose in ways she couldn't imagine. Her first challenge came in the form of an unexpected pregnancy. It was the result of her time in Johnny's house that would force her to confront questions of motherhood, protection, and the cyclical nature of trauma.

The system that had failed to protect her now viewed her through a new lens: a high-risk mother-to-be with a history of addiction and instability. As she fought to maintain custody of her unborn child, Michele discovered that breaking free from violence was only the first step in a longer journey toward healing and justice.

The pregnancy test's positive result shattered Michele's carefully constructed recovery plan. Sitting on the cold tile of her halfway house bathroom, she stared at the two pink lines that represented both her greatest fear and, potentially, her salvation.

"Approximately sixteen weeks," Dr. Winters confirmed during an emergency appointment. "Given your medical history and the circumstances... we should discuss all your options."

But Michele had already made her decision. In that first moment of revelation, her mother's voice had been crystal clear: "This is your chance to break the cycle, baby. To give the love you received from me."

The challenges began immediately. Her status as a key witness in ongoing trafficking investigations made traditional prenatal care complicated. Every medical appointment required security protocols. Each ultrasound technician had to be thoroughly vetted. Even her prenatal vitamins were checked for tampering.

"You're high-risk in more ways than one," Lisa Chen explained, still serving as her primary protection detail. "Johnny's network has people everywhere, and a baby gives them leverage."

The father's identity was a brutal uncertainty. Given the nature of her exploitation, there were multiple possibilities. None of them were comforting in any way. The prosecution team worried that this development might affect her credibility on the stand.

"They'll use this to discredit you," Martinez warned during a strategy session. "Paint you as unreliable, promiscuous, unfit."

"I've been painted as worse," Michele responded, one hand resting on her growing belly. "But this baby is mine. Just mine. They don't get to use him or her against me."

Her tenacity was tested when the Department of Family Services became involved. Her history of addiction, combined with her status as a trafficking survivor, triggered automatic oversight. A social worker named Karen Matthews was assigned to evaluate her fitness as a mother.

"Let's talk about your support system," Karen began their first meeting, flipping through Michele's extensive file. "And your plans for maintaining sobriety while parenting."

The irony wasn't lost on Michele. The same system that had failed to protect her from Harold now claimed to have a hold of power over her own child's future. But this time, she had allies.

Dr. Cohen helped her develop a comprehensive parenting plan that addressed both practical concerns and trauma-informed care. The prosecution team provided documentation of her cooperation and recovery progress. Even Dr. Winters wrote detailed medical reports supporting her capability to parent.

"You're not the same person who came into my trauma unit," Dr. Winters noted during a check-up. "You're choosing to live now, not just survive."

The unborn child provided the support that Michele needed the most, for the pregnancy itself became a kind of therapy. Each kick, each heartbeat on the monitor, each small development represented hope—something Michele had thought long lost in Johnny's house. She attended parenting classes, joined support groups for recovering mothers, and began intensive trauma therapy focused on breaking generational cycles of abuse. She did not just want to *show* that she was trying to become a better person, fit to raise a child. But she actually wanted to become that person for the sake of that child and the love her mother Glenda had instilled in her.

But the past wasn't finished with her. Seven months into

her pregnancy, Michele received news that would test everything she'd built: Harold was seeking contact. His latest appeal had been denied, and he claimed to want to make amends before she became a mother herself.

Harold's letter arrived on a Tuesday, delivered by his attorney rather than regular mail. The envelope sat untouched on Michele's kitchen table for three days while she wrestled with its implications. Dr. Cohen agreed to be present when she finally opened it.

"Remember," Dr. Cohen cautioned, "you have the power here. You choose how much access he gets to your life, if any."

The letter itself was twelve pages long, written with Harold's very own hands. It was a detail that made Michele's hands shake. Once the letter was opened, she read that he had written about finding God in prison, about understanding his failures as a father, about wanting to be a grandfather to her child. However, the words failed to have an impact on her, for each word seemed calculated to exploit her vulnerability.

"He's dying," his attorney explained during a follow-up meeting. "Cancer. He wants to make things right before he goes."

Michele thought of her mother, of how Harold had denied Glenda access to proper medical care, of how she'd died without the chance to see her daughter grow up. The symmetry was not lost on her.

"No," she decided finally. "He doesn't get to use his death to manipulate me or my child. That's not how this works."

This decision marked a turning point in her recovery. For

the first time, she was choosing to protect not just herself but the future she carried. Her therapy sessions shifted focus from processing past trauma to preparing for the challenges of protective parenting. She was finally healing.

"You're going to parent differently," Dr. Cohen explained. "Your hypervigilance, which can be debilitating in some contexts, might actually serve you well in keeping your child safe. The key is balance."

The final months of pregnancy brought new complications. Her blood pressure spiked dangerously, requiring bed rest. The stress of ongoing legal proceedings—both the trafficking case and Harold's attempts at contact—took its toll on her body.

During this time, an unexpected ally emerged. Amanda, Harold's former wife, reached out through official channels. She had divorced Harold years ago and wanted to testify about his abuse patterns to support Michele's case for complete separation.

"I was wrong," Amanda's statement read. "I was young and brainwashed, and I helped him hurt you. I can't undo that, but I can help protect your baby from him."

Labor began three weeks early, triggered by another spike in blood pressure. The delivery room became a secured zone, with Lisa Chen personally vetting every medical professional who entered. Michele fought through twenty-six hours of labor, refusing an epidural—her first completely drug-free experience of pain in years.

"I need to feel everything," she insisted when Dr. Winters

pushed for pain management. "I need to know I can do this on my own strength."

After hours and hours of struggle, the moment of joy finally knocked on Michele's door. Her daughter was born at 3:47 am. The baby was tiny but fierce, with a head full of dark hair just like Glenda's. When the nurse placed her on Michele's chest, the world shifted on its axis. Everything she'd survived, every horror she'd endured, suddenly had new context.

"Hello, Grace," she whispered, the name coming to her as naturally as breathing. "I've been waiting for you."

Nevertheless, the peaceful moment was short-lived. Within hours of Grace's birth, Michele received the first threat. A bouquet of black roses was delivered to the maternity ward, the card reading simply: "Johnny sends his congratulations."

The response was immediate. Grace was moved to the secure nursery, hospital security was doubled, and Michele's room was placed under 24-hour surveillance. Detective Morgan personally organized police protection for their eventual discharge.

But the greatest threat came from an unexpected direction. A routine drug screening of Grace's blood work— standard procedure for infants of former addicts—showed trace amounts of substances that shouldn't have been present.

"Someone tampered with your IV during labor," Dr. Winters concluded after reviewing the results. "We need to move you both immediately."

The safe house where Michele and Grace were relocated was a small ranch-style home on the outskirts of town. Every window was fitted with security sensors, and every door was reinforced with additional locks. For Michele, it felt uncomfortably familiar. It was just another house where safety meant imprisonment.

The first few weeks with Grace tested everything Michele had learned about managing her trauma responses. Every unexpected noise sent her into high alert. She developed a complex system of checking and rechecking locks, windows, and Grace's breathing that consumed hours of each day.

"This isn't paranoia," Dr. Cohen assured her during an emergency session, Grace sleeping peacefully in her carrier. "Your hypervigilance kept you alive in dangerous situations. Now we need to calibrate it for motherhood."

But the calibration was no less challenging. Michele struggled to sleep even when Grace did. Her mind was in a constant cycle of possible threats and escape scenarios. She now brought into use what her mother had done for her and the future that she'd have. She began documenting everything. She knew this could help her in ways she didn't understand in that moment. The documentation included feeding times, diaper changes, and sleep patterns. Each detail was noted with the same meticulous attention she'd once used to track drug inventories.

Something about it all did not sit right with Michele, though. "I'm becoming Harold," she confessed during one particularly difficult therapy session. "Controlling everything, writing everything down, always watching. I'm turning into the monster my mother and I had always tried to run away from."

Dr. Cohen's response shifted Michele's perspective. "Harold monitored to control and harm. You're monitoring to protect and nurture. Same behavior, completely different intent. The question is: how do we help you find balance?"

In all that chaos, the anchor became finding a balance. That balance began with small steps. Michele learned to distinguish between necessary vigilance and anxiety-driven compulsions. She created safe spaces within the safe house—corners and nooks where she could sit with Grace without having her back to a door or window.

Grace was not going to leave her mother alone in the fight. Though a baby, she proved to be an unexpected guide in this journey. Her innocent responses to the world, her delight in sunlight through windows Michele kept curtained, and her fascination with the sounds Michele flinched at gradually helped reshape her mother's perception of threat versus safety.

"Watch her," Dr. Cohen encouraged. "Babies have natural instincts for danger. When Grace is relaxed, try to let yourself relax, too. Let her teach you how to feel safe again."

The mother in Michele allowed herself to rely on her baby. So, it was not long before she would see some change and then came a breakthrough. It came during a midnight feeding. Grace had awakened hungry, and Michele was running through her usual security checks before settling into nurse. Suddenly, she caught her reflection in the window—a mirror of her mother, Glenda, from one of her earliest memories.

"Your grandmother would sing to you," Michele whispered to Grace. "Even when things were bad, she would sing."

That night, Michele sang for the first time since Montana. Her voice was rusty, the lullaby imperfect, but Grace's peaceful expression unleashed something locked inside her. Tears flowed as she sang, grieving for her mother while celebrating this new chance at maternal love.

Physical contact presented another challenge. Years of abuse had left Michele defensive about touch, but Grace needed constant holding, skin-to-skin contact, the intimate closeness of nursing. Each interaction required Michele to push through trauma responses, unlocking the soft mother's love in her.

"Your body remembers everything," her trauma-informed lactation consultant explained. "But it can learn new patterns. Every positive touch with Grace helps rewrite those neural pathways."

Michele began keeping a different kind of journal now. It was no longer about just tracking Grace's development but documenting her own growth as a mother. She noted the first time she managed to take a shower while Grace napped without checking on her every minute. The first time she enjoyed a thunderstorm with Grace instead of treating it as a security threat. The first time she let someone else — though carefully vetted, hold Grace without hovering.

"Dear Mom," she wrote one night, "I think I finally understand what you meant about love being stronger than fear. Grace is teaching me how to be brave in a whole new way."

The attachment process between Michele and Grace developed in ways she'd never expected.. While most mothers worried about bonding with their newborns, Michele's challenge was managing the intensity of her connection. Her hypervigilance transformed into an almost supernatural awareness of Grace's needs.

"You're attuned to her breathing patterns," the pediatrician noted during a check-up. "You know when she's about to cry before she makes a sound. These are actually positive adaptations of your trauma responses."

The healing and learning were not complete, though. Michele worked with Dr. Cohen to understand this transformation. Her sessions now included Grace, allowing the therapist to observe their interaction and help Michele distinguish between protective instincts and trauma reactions.

"When you check the locks three times, that's trauma," Dr. Cohen explained. "When you sense Grace's fever before it spikes, that's maternal instinct. We're learning to trust the right signals."

The journal Michele kept became more nuanced:

Day 147: I realized today I can tell the difference between Grace's "hungry" cry and her "tired" cry. Mom used to say she could do the same with me. Is this genetic? Or did we both develop this hyperawareness from living in danger? Either way, I'm using it to help, not hurt.

Day 183: Let Sarah (nurse from the witness protection team) hold Grace for 20 minutes without watching her hands. Progress? Still noted all exits and potential weapons in the room, but didn't feel the need to reclaim Grace immediately. Dr. C says this is balance.

Trust came in small increments. Michele learned to build a network of carefully vetted supporters—medical professionals, protection team members, fellow survivors in her support group. Each person was assessed not just for security risks but for their understanding of trauma-informed care.

"Your boundaries aren't walls," Dr. Cohen reminded her. "They're filters, letting in what Grace needs while keeping out what could harm her."

There was a blend of survival skills and maternal instincts that helped Michele become a better parent with each passing day. She used that blend to teach Grace baby sign language early, understanding the importance of communication when words might be dangerous. She developed games that incorporated awareness of her surroundings, turning her own hypervigilance into age-appropriate safety lessons.

But as Grace approached her first birthday, new threats emerged. Johnny's network, though diminished by ongoing prosecutions, hadn't forgotten them. The first warning came through official channels—a threat assessment from witness protection noting increased activity around their case.

Then Grace's father resurfaced. DNA testing had confirmed paternity, and he was demanding rights. He was backed by expensive lawyers and connections to Johnny's remaining organization. The legal documents arrived on Grace's first birthday, turning the celebration into a crisis.

"He's using the system against you," Martinez warned during an emergency meeting. "Just like Harold did. They've learned it's more effective than violence."

Michele's response surprised everyone, including herself. Instead of panic, she felt a cold, clear fury. This wasn't just about her survival anymore; it was about breaking the cycle for Grace.

"My mother couldn't beat the system," she told her legal team. "She didn't have the resources or support. But I'm not alone, and I'm not running. We're fighting this."

The decision to fight set in motion a series of events that would test everything Michele had built. The custody battle exposed her to new forms of trauma—character assassination in court, invasive psychological evaluations, constant scrutiny of her parenting.

The courthouse bathroom mirror reflected a different Michele than the one who had fled Harold's house years ago. Her eyes held steel rather than fear, her posture spoke of determination instead of defeat. Grace's father might have money and connections, but Michele had something stronger—a mother's resolve to protect her child and a survivor's knowledge of how to fight impossible odds.

As she straightened her jacket and checked her court documents one last time, Michele thought of Sandra, of her mother, of all the women who had sacrificed to get her to this moment. Their strength flowed through her, combining with her own hard-won wisdom. She had to win this and not just fight for the sake of all those who had built a road for her.

"Ready?" Lisa Chen asked, holding the bathroom door.

Michele nodded, thinking of Grace safe with her protection team. "They tried to bury us," she said quietly.

"They didn't know we were seeds."

The custody battle lasted eighteen months, draining Michele's resources but strengthening her resolve. Each court appearance revealed more about the systemic failures that enabled abusers to maintain control through legal means. She began documenting everything—not just for her case, but for others who might follow.

"Your Honor," Michele addressed the court during a crucial hearing, "this isn't just about Grace. This is about every child born to a mother trying to escape violence. Every time we allow abusers to use the courts as weapons, we fail these children."

Her words caught the attention of Angela Richardson, a domestic violence advocate observing the proceedings. After court, Angela approached Michele with a proposition that would change both their lives.

"You understand something most people don't," Angela said, sharing coffee in the courthouse café. "The system isn't broken—it's functioning exactly as designed. To protect power, not people."

Michele thought of all the women she'd met in support groups, each fighting similar battles with different faces. "So how do we change it?"

"We start with your story," Angela replied. "But we make it about more than just you."

The idea took root during Grace's nap times. Michele began writing. It was first in her journal, then in more structured forms. She documented the patterns she'd observed.

It included how abusers utilized family courts, how trafficking networks infiltrated legitimate systems, and how poverty and trauma created cycles of vulnerability.

Dr. Cohen helped her see the larger implications of her experiences. "Your perspective is unique," she noted during a session. "You've seen these systems from every angle. You've done so as a child victim, as a trafficked woman, as a recovering mother fighting for custody. That knowledge has power."

The transition from personal survival to advocacy wasn't smooth. During one particularly difficult court session, Grace's father's attorney attempted to use Michele's emerging public voice against her.

"Isn't it true," the lawyer demanded, "that you're exploiting these proceedings for attention? Using your daughter's situation to build a platform?"

Michele's response silenced the courtroom: "I'm speaking out because silence protects abusers. Every parent in this room knows you'd walk through fire to protect your child. I'm choosing to walk through shame, through trauma, through character assassination. And bold of you to assume that this is just for Grace. This isn't just for her but for every child whose parent couldn't fight back."

The judge's ruling, when it finally came, reflected a small but significant shift in the system. Grace would remain in Michele's full custody, with strict protective orders against her father. More importantly, the judge cited Michele's advocacy work as evidence of her commitment to breaking cycles of abuse.

The survivor advocacy center Michele helped establish

became a testament to everything she'd learned about healing and protection. Located in a renovated Victorian mansion, its architecture deliberately inverted the power dynamics she'd experienced in Johnny's properties. Where he had created spaces designed to disorient and control, Michele ensured every room offered clear sightlines and multiple exits. Natural light flooded through large windows, and security measures were obvious rather than hidden. It was all to empower rather than threaten.

"We're not hiding anymore," she explained during the center's opening ceremony, Grace secure in a carrier against her chest. "Survival shouldn't mean living in shadows."

The program she developed with Angela combined Michele's precise understanding of trafficking operations with trauma-informed care practices. Lessons that she learned were reflected in each aspect. Financial literacy classes taught survivors to reclaim control over money without triggering memories of keeping Johnny's books; parenting support groups helped mothers like her navigate the complex intersection of trauma and childcare.

Grace's presence in the center became part of its healing environment. Now three years old, she moved through the spaces with natural confidence, offering a silent declaration of the possibility of raising children without fear. Michele watched her daughter's interactions with careful attention, learning as much about healing from Grace's natural resilience as from any therapy session.

"Your daughter treats everyone like they're safe," one new resident observed, watching Grace share toys in the center's communal space.

"Because here they are," Michele responded. "And eventually, they'll believe it too."

The transformation of Michele's trauma into expertise drew attention from law enforcement and policymakers. Her testimony before state legislative committees helped shape new laws protecting trafficking survivors' parental rights. The detailed documentation systems she'd developed—born from years of keeping Johnny's ledgers—became models for case management in survivor support programs.

But the work extracted its own price. Each new case triggered memories. Each success story reminded her of those still trapped. The balance between advocacy and personal healing remained delicate, complicated by the ongoing threats from diminished but persistent trafficking networks.

"You can't save everyone," Dr. Cohen reminded her during their now-monthly check-ins. "But you're changing the system that failed to save you."

The breakthrough in this regard was not going to come announced. It came unexpectedly during a late-night session with a new resident. The young woman, barely eighteen, had a familiar look in her eyes She had the same desperate calculation Michele had once lived with. As they talked, Michele found herself sharing not just survival strategies but hope.

"My mother died trying to protect me," she told the girl, Grace, sleeping peacefully in the next room. "But she also showed me how to live. That's the real legacy. It is not just surviving, but building something better from the wreckage."

That night, watching Grace sleep, Michele began writing

again. Not just documentation or testimony but a different kind of legacy—a roadmap for her daughter, explaining the choices that had shaped their lives. It became both memoir and manual, a way to ensure that even if history repeated itself, Grace would have what Michele hadn't: understanding.

My Dearest Grace,

There are things you need to know about where you come from and about the strength that runs in your blood. Your grandmother, Glenda, taught me that love is both a sword and a shield. In you, I see her courage blooming anew...

The manuscript grew alongside the advocacy center's programs. Michele's precise memory once used to track human suffering, now preserved stories of transformation. Each chapter balanced darkness with light, documenting not just how systems fail but how they can be rebuilt.

The center's success attracted attention from national organizations, leading to requests for Michele to help establish similar programs across the country. Each new project built on lessons learned, creating a network of support that would have saved her mother, might have caught her before Johnny's web, and could prevent countless others from similar fates.

"This is how we fight back," she explained to her expanding team. "Not just by helping survivors escape, but by changing what they're escaping into."

Grace started kindergarten the same week Michele testified before Congress. The timing felt symbolic—her daughter taking her first independent steps into the world as Michele helped shape policies to make that world safer. The contrast between Grace's innocent excitement about school and Michele's understanding of lurking dangers created a new kind of challenge.

"How do we protect them without teaching them fear?" she asked during a parent support group at the center.

The answers came from unexpected places. Grace herself showed Michele daily how to balance awareness with joy. The survivors working at the center demonstrated that healing wasn't about forgetting danger but about choosing to live fully despite it.

Five years after Grace's birth, Michele stood at a podium accepting a national advocacy award. Her daughter sat in the front row, dark hair and bright eyes so like Glenda's, holding Mr. Hoppy—now a third-generation symbol of survival.

"Legacy isn't just what we leave behind," Michele told the audience. "It's what we choose to transform. Every survivor who reclaims their story, every child born into freedom instead of fear, and every system changed by our collective voice. For these are the true monuments to those we lost along the way."

The light through the convention center's windows caught Grace's smile. For a moment, Michele saw three generations of strength reflected. The first was Glenda's protective love. The second was her own hard-won wisdom, and the third was Grace's natural ability to find joy in a world her mother and grandmother had died making safer.

Their true legacy was not just survival. It was very much a transformation. It was not just an escape, but it was also a revolution. It was not just healing. It was hope.

Chapter 7:
Ripples of Change

The news reached Michele on a Tuesday morning. Harold had died in prison. The email from the victim notification system was clinically brief, for there were only three sentences. The words confirmed his death from aggressive cancer, the same disease that had taken her mother. Michele sat in her office at the advocacy center, where Grace's artwork decorated the walls around her. It felt as though the weight of circles was closing. A crayon drawing of butterflies emerged from cocoons that hung directly in her line of sight, Grace's latest metaphor for their work.

The notification had come while she was preparing for a meeting with state legislators about expanding survivor services. Michele found herself staring at the butterfly drawing, remembering the cold metal of Harold's handcuffs against her skin, the musty smell of his house, the sound of his voice calling her "princess." The memories no longer had the power to paralyze her, but they still carried weight, like stones in her pocket she'd learned to carry while walking.

"Are you going to the funeral?" Grace asked that evening, wise beyond her seven years of age. Her question carried no judgment, only curiosity about how adults navigated these complex waters of grief and trauma. They sat at their kitchen table, homework spread between them, the remnants of dinner pushed aside to make room for conversation.

"No, baby," Michele answered, running her fingers through her daughter's dark hair—so like Glenda's. "But we're going to do something else. Something that matters more." She pulled Grace closer, breathing in the scent of her strawberry shampoo, as she found strength in the solid warmth of her daughter's presence.

That night, after Grace fell asleep, Michele sat at her computer crafting an email to her network of survivors and advocates. Her fingers hovered over the keyboard as she searched for the right words:

*Dear Warriors,

Today, I learned that one of my abusers died in prison. The system would say justice was served—he was caught, convicted, and died behind bars. But we know justice isn't just about punishment. It's about transformation. It's about ensuring that for every person who causes harm, there are dozens of us working to heal it.

I'm organizing a candlelight vigil. Not for him but for all of us. For every child still trapped, for every survivor still fighting, for every voice still waiting to be heard. Will you join me?*

The responses flooded in immediately. Survivors she'd worked with over the years, advocates who'd become friends, even some law enforcement officers who'd learned to trust their approach. Each message carried the same theme:

We'll be there.

We stand with you.

Your pain matters.

Your healing matters more.

Instead of attending Harold's funeral, Michele organized the candlelight vigil at the advocacy center. The turnout exceeded all expectations. Hundreds gathered in the parking lot, their flames creating a sea of light that reminded Michele of stars. She recognized many faces from years of advocacy work—Amanda, older now and sober, carrying her own stories of survival; Detective Martinez, who'd helped build the case against Johnny; Sarah from the hospital, now heading their medical advocacy program.

"He didn't win," Amanda said simply, lighting her candle from Michele's. "None of them did." Her hands were steady now, free from the tremors of withdrawal that had once marked her early days of recovery. She wore her five-year sobriety chip on a chain around her neck, right next to a pendant matching the butterfly drawing on Michele's wall.

The vigil became a catalyst for unexpected change. Local news cameras captured the event, initially drawn by the size of the crowd, but staying for the stories. Michele hadn't planned to speak, but standing there surrounded by fellow survivors, she felt compelled to share the words that she had in her heart.

"My abuser died today," she began, her voice carrying across the hushed parking lot. "Society would say this is closure. But we know better, don't we? We know that healing doesn't come from a death notification. It comes from breaking the silence. It comes from turning pain into purpose. It comes from standing here, together, saying 'No more.'"

The media coverage drew attention to their work, but more importantly, it drew out new survivors. Women who had been silenced by shame or fear found their voices, inspired by Michele's public acknowledgment of her past. Each new story that emerged validated their approach that healing happened not in isolation but in the community.

The advocacy center expanded rapidly in the months following the vigil. They added specialized programs for children of abuse survivors, something Michele had been pushing for since Grace first started asking questions about their work. The approach, shaped by her experience mothering Grace, emphasized understanding rather than forgetting. She recognized that children needed context for their family's struggles—not to carry the burden of trauma but to understand their own resilience.

"Our children need to know where they come from," she explained during a training session for new staff, Grace's artwork serving as backdrop to her presentation. "Not to carry our trauma, but to understand their own strength. When we hide our healing from them, we risk teaching them that some parts of ourselves should stay in shadow."

The children's program took shape under Michele's careful guidance. They created age-appropriate support groups, art therapy sessions, and educational programs about healthy relationships. Grace, though still young, became an unofficial mentor to other survivors' children, showing them through example that their parents' past didn't define their future.

"My mom helps people find their brave," Grace explained to a new child in the program, offering her favorite colored pencils. "Sometimes being brave means telling your story, and sometimes it means drawing pictures of how you feel."

The ripples of their work spread further than Michele could have imagined. Her testimony before Congress, built on years of meticulous documentation and firsthand experience, led to groundbreaking legislation protecting trafficking survivors' parental rights. She stood before the judiciary committee, her mother's strength in her spine, and spoke truth to power.

"The current system punishes survivors twice," she testified. "First through the trauma of trafficking, then by using that trauma to deny us custody of our children. We're labeled as unfit parents because of crimes committed against us. This has to stop."

The documentation methods she'd developed, which were born out of years of keeping Johnny's books, became standard practice in survivor support programs nationwide. Her systematic approach to tracking cases, identifying patterns, and building evidence trails revolutionized how advocacy organizations operated.

But the most significant change came unexpectedly. A series of high-profile trafficking cases brought renewed attention to Johnny's network, still operating in diminished form from prison. Michele's detailed records, combined with new evidence, led to a wave of additional convictions that reached into unexpected corners of power.

"Your mother's original documentation helped us connect the dots," Detective Martinez explained, now heading a specialized trafficking task force. "She started this snowball rolling years ago. You're just helping it gain momentum." He spread case files across Michele's desk, each one representing another link in the chain they were steadily dismantling.

The investigation revealed how deeply the corruption ran. Police officers, judges, and child services workers were all complicit in maintaining trafficking networks. Each revelation validated Glenda's paranoia, proving her careful documentation had been not madness but methodology. Michele found herself revisiting her mother's journals with new understanding, seeing now how Glenda had been mapping a system no one else wanted to acknowledge.

"Look at this," Michele showed Dr. Cohen during a session, bringing one of Glenda's notebooks. "She wasn't just recording what happened to us. She was tracking patterns, identifying connections, building a case. She knew no one would believe her, so she documented everything."

Dr. Cohen, still a steady presence in Michele's healing journey, helped her process the complex emotions of discovering her mother's hidden purpose. "Your mother was fighting in the only way she could," she observed. "And now you're finishing what she started, but with resources and support she never had."

Michele's role shifted from witness to expert consultant. Her understanding of how trafficking operations infiltrated legitimate systems proved invaluable in dismantling similar networks across the country. The same precision that had once made her valuable to Johnny now helped destroy everything he'd built. There was poetry to it that didn't escape her—using the skills of her captivity to ensure others' freedom.

The advocacy center developed new protocols based on their expanding understanding of trafficking networks. They created training programs for law enforcement, healthcare workers, and social services staff. Michele insisted on survivor leadership at every level.

"We're not just consultants," she would explain in training sessions. "We're experts. Our experience isn't a liability. It is, in fact, our greatest asset. We understand these systems because we survived them. Now we're using that knowledge to change them."

Their approach gained recognition in academic circles. Michele collaborated with researchers to document their methods, contributing to a growing body of evidence supporting survivor-led advocacy. She found herself navigating new territory—academic conferences, peer-reviewed journals, research partnerships.

Grace turned eight the year Michele published her first academic paper on trauma-informed survivor advocacy. The publication party at the center became a celebration of multiple victories—personal, professional, and systemic. The paper, "Breaking Chains: Survivor-Led Approaches to Trafficking Prevention" would go on to influence policy in multiple states.

The celebration brought together their ever-growing community. Amanda, now working as a peer counselor at the center, brought her famous recovery brownies. Detective Martinez showed up with his whole family, his daughters close to Grace's age. Sarah from the hospital presented Michele with a framed copy of the paper's first page, signatures of support from the entire medical staff surrounding it.

"My mom keeps trying to change the world," Grace announced to the gathered crowd, her voice carrying the same quiet strength that had once marked Glenda's rare moments of peace. "And it's working."

Michele touched the locket at her neck, feeling the familiar weight of the two photos inside—Glenda and Grace, grandmother and granddaughter, connected by more than blood. The waves of their story continued to spread, touching lives they would never know, creating changes they could only imagine.

That night, after the celebration, Michele found Grace in her office, studying the wall of success stories—photos of survivors who'd gone on to become advocates, lawyers, counselors, each one a ripple becoming a wave.

"Mom," Grace said, pointing to a blank space on the wall, "we should leave room for more stories."

Michele smiled, recognizing in her daughter's words the essence of their work: the understanding that every ending was also a beginning, every ripple the start of new possibilities. She thought about Harold's death notice, still sitting in her email inbox. His ending had created space for so many new beginnings.

"You know what, baby?" Michele said, wrapping an arm around Grace's shoulders. "I think we're going to need a bigger wall."

Together, they stood in the quiet office, surrounded by

evidence of lives transformed—Grace's artwork, survivor success stories, academic achievements, and that empty space full of possibility. Michele thought about all the circles closing and opening: Harold's death, her mother's journals finding purpose, Grace growing into her role in their movement.

She recognized that the impact would extend long beyond this moment. Each survivor who embraced their voice would generate new waves of change, every story shared would inspire others to tell their own, and each victory would create opportunities for newcomers to thrive. Change occurs not through dramatic gestures or fleeting moments, but through the accumulation of countless small swells that unite to forge significant waves of transformation.

Michele pulled Grace closer, breathing in the scent of strawberry shampoo and childhood, feeling the steady beat of her daughter's heart against her side. In that moment, she understood with perfect clarity what her mother had known all along: love was stronger than fear, the truth was stronger than silence, and the currents of change could never be stopped once they began.

Chapter 8:
Sparks Create Change

The conference room was packed. Every seat was filled with survivors, advocates, and service providers. Through the floor-to-ceiling windows of the United Nations building, Manhattan sparkled in the early morning light, for there were thousands of tiny lights like the sparks they'd been creating for decades. Michele stood at the podium, one hand touching the locket that held Grace's picture, the other steady on her prepared remarks. The audience expected another sad story about trafficking and abuse. What they got instead was a blueprint for how individual sparks could ignite a revolution.

"We talk about sparks of hope," Michele began, her voice carrying the weight of hard-won wisdom. "But a spark without fuel is just a moment of light that fades into darkness. Hope without action is just another way to keep us quiet. Today, we're not here to share stories of survival. We're here to show how every spark of resistance, every flash of defiance, every glimmer of courage can combine to create lasting change."

In the back of the room, Angela smiled, remembering their first spark which was nothing more than a desperate midnight phone call, two survivors recognizing each other's pain, deciding that survival wasn't enough. Their vision had grown from that single spark into a blazing movement. From there, a network of survivors turned activists as each one of them carried their own light into the darkness they'd escaped.

The presentation screen behind Michele was illuminated with evidence. There were arrest records, court documents, protection order violations, and whatnot. Each piece represented a spark of truth that had helped light the way for others. But it was the next slide that caught everyone's attention. It was a complex flowchart that showed how trafficking networks utilized legitimate businesses, legal systems, and social services gaps to maintain control over victims.

"This is what darkness looks like when you shine a light on it," Michele explained, her voice steady despite the trembling in her hands. "Every point of failure, every loophole, every shadow where exploitation hides. And this—" she clicked again, revealing a network of survivor-led organizations, safe houses, and advocacy groups spanning five continents, each location marked by a point of light, "—this is what happens when sparks combine to create change."

She moved through the presentation, showing how each small victory had ignited others. The Golden Rail's transformation from an exploitation hub to a resource center glimmered similar conversions worldwide. Each converted space became a beacon, drawing survivors toward safety and inspiring more transformations.

"A single spark can start a forest fire," Michele said, "but it can also light a beacon of hope, illuminate a path in darkness, or signal others to safety. The spark itself isn't good or bad. It's what we choose to do with it that matters."

Grace, now twelve, had inherited this understanding of sparks. Her youth program, "Spark Seeds," taught children how to recognize their own power to create change. The program spread through schools like wildfire, each child becoming a potential spark of transformation.

Their impact grew beyond numbers, though the statistics burned bright:

- Seventy percent reduction in recidivism rates among trafficking survivors in their programs
- Eighty-five percent success rate in custody cases for survivor parents
- Landmark legislation passed in thirty-seven states
- Over ten thousand survivors transitioned from victims to advocates
- Millions in seized trafficking assets redirected to spark new programs
  - ➤ But the real legacy lived in the small moments—each one a spark that could ignite change:
- A mother reuniting with her children, sparking hope in other fighting parents
- A survivor celebrating sobriety, igniting possibility in those still struggling
- A victim finding their voice in court, lighting the way for others to speak
- A child learning to set boundaries, becoming a spark of prevention
  - ➤ Michele detailed their innovative approaches, each designed to create new sparks:
- Trauma-informed legal advocacy programs teaching survivors to light their own paths
- Survivor-led investigation teams turning pain into purpose

- Child-centered family reunification protocols sparking generational healing
- Economic empowerment initiatives igniting financial independence
- International training networks spreading sparks across borders

During a landmark testimony before Congress earlier that year, Michele had created a spark that turned into a wildfire. When a senator questioned the reliability of trafficking survivors as witnesses, she'd departed from her prepared statement:

"You're right to question us," she had said, her voice steady. "We've lied. We've stolen. We've done whatever it took to survive. But here's what you need to understand. Those very skills, the ones used to dismiss us, are what make us experts at identifying how these systems fail. We know every crack because we fell through them. We know every loophole because they were used against us. And now we're using that knowledge to light the way for others."

The applause in the UN conference room swelled as Michele played that clip. She waited for the room to quiet before continuing.

"Twenty years ago, I was a single spark—a trafficking victim trying to regain custody of my daughter. Today, we're a bonfire of change. Twenty years ago, I kept detailed records of my exploitation because I didn't know how else to survive. Today, those same skills have helped ignite systematic change across the globe."

She brought up a map showing their global impact—

points of light representing each resource center, each survivor-led program, each legislative victory. The lights clustered and spread like stars across continents, a constellation of change they'd created together.

That evening, back in their hotel room, Grace helped Michele prepare for the next day's workshops. "Mom," she said, sorting through presentation materials, "do you ever wonder about the first spark? The moment everything started to change?"

Michele touched her locket, thinking of Glenda's quiet resistance, of Sandra's sacrifice, of every small act of defiance that had led to this moment. "Change doesn't come from one spark, baby. It comes from all of us choosing to keep our lights burning, even when the darkness feels overwhelming."

Twenty years into their work, Michele found herself returning to where it all began. It was the small chapel in Montana where her mother was buried. Grace stood beside her, both of them placing fresh flowers on Glenda's grave.

"Your grandmother," Michele told Grace, touching their matching lockets, "was the first spark. She taught me that love burns brighter than fear. She kept her light alive in the darkest times so that one day, we could help light the way for others."

That evening, at a ceremony honoring their organization's work, Michele shared her final reflection.

"We often talk about breaking cycles of abuse, addiction, and trauma. But maybe it's not about breaking cycles at all. Maybe it's about creating new sources of light—sparks of healing, of empowerment, of transformation. Every survivor who heals becomes a new spark of possibility. Every voice that speaks the truth ignites more voices. Every small act of resistance can spark revolutionary change."

Grace stepped forward then, taking her mother's hand, their matching lockets catching the light. In that moment, they represented everything their movement stood for—the power of transformed pain becoming light, the strength of generational healing creating new sparks, and the endless possibility of change.

The fire they ignited would keep growing, not as something harmful but as a source of change. Each spark represented a new beginning, every change brought hope, and each bit of hope shone a light for others to follow.

As the applause faded and the audience began to disperse, Michele noticed Grace studying the global impact map still displayed on the screen, each point of light representing countless stories of transformation.

"Ready to go home?" Michele asked.

Grace squeezed her hand. "Not yet, Mom. There are still more sparks to create."

Michele smiled, recognizing in her daughter's words the truth that had guided their entire journey. Change wasn't just about the sparks they'd already created but about all the potential sparks still waiting to be kindled. Each generation carried the flame forward in their own way, adding new light to their constellation of change.

This was their legacy. This was their testimony. This was how sparks created change—one light at a time until the darkness had nowhere left to hide.

www.ingramcontent.com/pod-product-compliance
Lightning Source LLC
Chambersburg PA
CBHW051221120626
46547CB00013B/1459